PAT THE DOG AND KILL THE PARENTS!

A book of professional writing secrets for young people

By

Bryony Pearce

For Beth Walsh, Elea Weaver, Chloe-Marie Olutawula

and all the inspiring young writers out there!

Other books by Bryony Pearce

Angel's Fury

The Weight of Souls

Phoenix Rising

Phoenix Burning

Wavefunction

Windrunner's Daughter

Savage Island

Cruel Castle

Raising Hell

The Girl on the Platform

Little Rumours

Introduction

I don't remember what made me want to become a writer, because it's always been my dream. For as long as I can remember I've loved to read, so I suspect it was the moment I discovered that books were written by actual people and that it was a real job that you could have.

When I was in primary school, we didn't have a television - if I wanted to be entertained, I would read, or tell stories. My family also moved around *a lot* and I worked out, fairly early on, that being a storyteller gave me a way to make friends. I remember when I was nine, telling ghost stories to the other children.

One particularly memorable tale involved a little girl who had died from the black death. In my story she roamed the village at night, looking for children. If you saw her, she would take you to be her playmate for the rest of eternity.

For a while I was a popular playtime obsession until some of the other kids had nightmares, their parents complained, and I was banned from storytelling in the playground!

Come with me if you want to live ... forever

Thankfully, that didn't stop me. I've been writing stories my whole life and now I'm a published author. I write novels for young adults (some have won awards, you may even have heard of me), as well as thrillers for adults and short stories for anthologies.

I also work as a creative writing teacher. Which means I help people who dream of becoming published novelists, like I once did.

One of the things I have noticed while teaching, is that there are some pieces of writing advice that, once you know about them, are easy to action and which make a piece of writing so much better. *But*, few wannabe writers actually know them!

So, why am I writing this book for *you?*

Well, I had some young writers get in touch asking for help. Very quickly I realised that these writers had talent and drive. The only thing holding them back was the fact that in school students simply aren't taught professional writing tricks (which, fair enough).

And I thought -Why should these amazing young writers be held back because of their age? Why not let them into all these writing secrets so that they can reach their full potential?

So, I wrote this book for young people who want to write like professionals. And yes, if you're a grown-up reading this, then you're very welcome into our space, you might have to duck a bit, cross your legs when you sit down. That's right.

Welcome.

Contents

I've written this book with a structure in mind, there's a logical sense to it. But that doesn't mean you have to start reading on page one and finish at the end! Use this contents page to find the bits that interest you, or which might help you *right now*. Dip in and out, I don't mind!

I've also included, along with my writing advice, links to videos, suggestions of other things to read, writing exercises, websites to visit ... so while you *can* just *read* this book, you can also be more interactive. Read it with a pencil and, if you have one, a tablet, beside you, make notes in the margins, turn down corners of interesting pages, bend the spine.

Have fun ...

Contents

The ideas bit

The importance of reading

(I know, I know, you *know* this!)

If you want to be a brilliant writer (which obviously you do - why else would you be here?) then you also have to be a reader.

You would be amazed how many people send me work to edit and then act surprised when I ask them what their favourite book in the same genre (category) is. It turns out that they can't tell me because *they don't read the genre they're writing* (grown-ups, right!). The first thing I do with these guys is send them a reading list!

Why would you want to *write* young adult literature (for example) if you don't like to *read* young adult literature? That's like being a chef who hates food, or a musician who hates music!

There are lots of reasons that reading in general is important. And there are lots of reasons that reading is essential to becoming a writer.

Why read?

You're here, so I'm guessing you know all the usual answers:

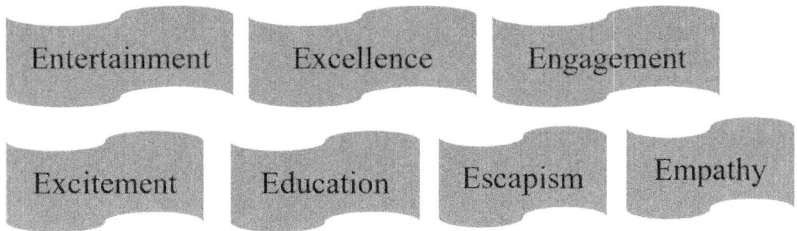

Look at all those lovely E words!

Did you also know that teenagers who read *FOR FUN* (that means outside the books you have to read for school), are more likely to end up in professional or managerial positions?

Did you know that teenagers who read *FOR FUN* do better in tests, are more empathetic and are better at public speaking?

So basically, if you read *FOR FUN*, you'll end up richer, nicer and more interesting - ***FACT!***

If you want to become a great writer, there are even more reasons to be a great reader.

1. **Reading other people's books gives *you* ideas.**

   'They' say that there are no more new ideas. According to Google (the fount of all wisdom) in 2020 there were -

   <u>*129,864,828*</u>

   (ALMOST 130 MILLION)

   different published books in all of modern history (some of these are mine, which is cool)!

   From which I can conclude that every idea that can possibly be had, has probably been had! Boy has met girl in every possible scenario. Boy has lost girl in every possible scenario and so on.

   So, it's okay to magpie ideas from other books you have read, TV shows or films you have watched, songs you have heard. *The key is to give the basic story (boy meets girl)* ***your own original spin***.

   Perhaps the boy is a ghost inhabiting the car in which he died, and the girl falls in love with him when she buys his old car. Perhaps the girl is a swimmer, and the boy is a merman. Perhaps the girl is an adventurer, and the boy is from a mysterious lost tribe and so on.

2. **Reading other people's books shows you what is already out there.**

Imagine that you spend ten years writing a book. You think it's the best thing ever. You don't read, of course, reading is for the masses. You are a *writer*.

Now your story is about a boy called Barry. Barry is a wizard, only he doesn't know it because he is raised in the human world by his cruel Aunt. When he gets an invitation to a wizard school called Bogsnorts, Barry is delighted, but then he has to face the evil magician who killed his parents: Mouldysnort!

… will this book ever be published?

You need to know what's already out there so that you don't inadvertently replicate it. You'd be amazed how many ideas I've had that I thought were brilliant and original. Then, after I've written a couple of chapters, I pick up a book and lo-and-behold, someone else has written the same story. Or I'm telling a friend my idea and they say, isn't that the storyline of X?

3. Reading other people's books shows you how to write ...

If you want to write a particular kind of book, it is useful to know how those books are written.

For example, when I decided to write my first YA (young adult) horror I read a selection of YA horror novels before I started (and no, I didn't sleep for a week afterwards).

You also need to know what kind of writing style suits a particular kind of book, for example, lots of description versus lots of fast-paced action.

Don't just read the kind of book you want to write though. If you want to write a science-fiction novel, then definitely read a lot of science-fiction, but also read romance, fantasy, horror, thriller, historical, dystopia etc.

Why? Because writers in other genres will still offer techniques you can learn.

You might not generally enjoy, for example, romance, but in reading a romance novel you might learn how to write excellent dialogue.

'I wish, as well as everybody else, to be perfectly happy; but like everybody else it must be in my own way.' (Sense and Sensibility, Jane Austen)

You might not enjoy historical, but in reading a historical novel you might learn how to do amazing world building.

It was the best of times, it was the worst of times, it was the age of wisdom, it was the age of foolishness, it was the epoch of belief, it was the epoch of incredulity, it was the season of light, it was the season of darkness, it was the spring of hope, it was the winter of despair. (Charles Dickens, A Tale of Two Cities)

You might not enjoy horror, but in reading a horror novel, you might learn how to create a creepy atmosphere.

There was a deliberate voluptuousness that was both thrilling and repulsive and as she arched her neck, she actually licked her lips, like an animal, till I could see in the moonlight the moisture. Then lapped the white, sharp teeth. (Bram Stoker, Dracula)

Fantasy might teach you description.

I watched her departure, as one watches a sunset. She went like a radiance through the dark wood, which was henceforth bright to me, from simply knowing that such a creature was in it. (George MacDonald, Phantastes)

Comedy might teach you timing.

Jeeves," I said. "A rummy communication has arrived. From Mr. Glossop."

"Indeed, sir?"

"I will read it to you. Handed in at Upper Bleaching. Message runs as follows:

When you come tomorrow, bring my football boots. Also, if humanly possible, Irish water-spaniel. Urgent. Regards. Tuppy.

"What do you make of that, Jeeves?"

15

"As I interpret the document, sir, Mr. Glossop wishes you, when you come tomorrow, to bring his football boots. Also, if humanly possible, an Irish water-spaniel. He hints that the matter is urgent, and sends his regards."

"Yes, that is how I read it. But why football boots?"

"Perhaps Mr. Glossop wishes to play football, sir."

(P.G. Wodehouse, Very Good, Jeeves!)

Realism might give you an amazing opening hook.

Grady's hands were round my throat and I was too weak to fight him off. I was going to die but I couldn't bring myself to care. (Bryony Pearce, Cruel Castle)

And so on …

When you read, pay attention to the bits you like and see if you can work out what the writer has done and how you can borrow their technique for your own work.

4. And how not to write.

Of course, when you're reading, you might *not* enjoy a book, or part of a book and that can help you too! Perhaps a writer does something that annoys you – well now you know not to do that in your own work. Or maybe the dialogue is terrible – can you work out what they're doing wrong and avoid it?

Ideas and Inspiration

If you're a young person reading this book, then congratulations, you have a big advantage over us old folk … your imagination. You haven't yet learned what isn't possible, which means that anything is. You probably already have so many ideas that sometimes you feel as if your brain is going to *explode.*

However, as someone with their own overflowing idea-pan, I know that sometimes you are faced with having to write something and … you're stuck. The ideas will not flow.

Sometimes you need to find a little inspiration, and this is where this section of the book comes in.

What is inspiration? There is a dictionary definition, which you can look up for yourself, don't be lazy! Then there's my definition, which is basically '***stubborn interest***'.

Imagine that you go into your school hall. In the centre of the floor there is …

a splatter of blood!

Now some people, we shall call them muggles, for want of a better word, will see that blood, shrug, and say …

'There's some blood … maybe I should call a cleaner.'

And then they will *forget about it*!

Writing wizards will see that drop of blood and say to themselves …

'Hey, that's blood! I wonder how it got there! Whose blood is it? What happened here? Was there a fight? Who had that fight? What started the fight? What happened to the winner and the loser? Where are they now? …'

Eventually the wizard will have built a whole story in their head from seeing that one drop of blood.

It doesn't have to be the true story of what happened – this isn't a book for forensic scientists! That thing you saw - that blood spatter, it interested you, you stubbornly held onto that interest and that *inspired a story.*

Inspiration is that moment when something interests you, but you don't let it go.

Which means that the things that interest you generally, are great material for generating writing ideas.

When I was young, I was fascinated by world mythology, especially Greek, Roman, Nordic, Aztec and Egyptian. I had a pile of books on myths and legends, death practices etc. So, when I came to write my first books, where did I go for inspiration? World mythology!

My first book involved reincarnation (Hindu) and fallen angels (Christian). My second book involved Egyptian Gods and ancient curses. Even my books that don't appear to contain world mythology (like *Savage Island*) secretly do (In *Savage Island*, Carmen is a modern Maenad).

All of your interests, from dancing to music, from stamp collecting to stargazing, can be sources of inspiration for stories!

Where else can you get ideas?

I've already mentioned that you can magpie ideas from other people's work (as long as you put your own original spin on them) but there are plenty of other potential sources of inspiration.

Try listening to the news, you'd be amazed how many novelists have taken their ideas from news stories.

Read history books – lots of writers get their ideas from real events that happened in the past. Booker Prize winner, Maggie O' Farrell, for example, wrote a story about the death of Shakespeare's son, *Hamnet*.

Look at some art — what do you think the story is behind the painting? How was the painter feeling, or experiencing when he created his art? The award-winning novel *Girl with a Pearl Earring* by Tracy Chevalier (later made into a film with Scarlet Johansson) is based on the oil painting *Girl with a Pearl Earring* by Johannes Vermeer (1665).

Read science magazines. The *New Scientist* is my personal favourite for idea generation. If you can't find a story idea in there, you can't find one anywhere!

Go to www.newscientist.com to see what kinds of articles are on there today.

A quick look at the headlines from 2nd Feb 2021 gives me such awesome story idea generators as:

How to spot alien megastructures.

Smart speakers could hear your heart beating from across the room.

Video game graphics card can simulate monkey brains.

Was it just luck that our species survived and the Denisovians didn't?

Fish recorded singing dawn chorus on reef just like birds.

Here is a real (completely awesome) New Scientist article from August 2012 …

Stone Age skull-smashers spark a cultural mystery!

An unusual cluster of Stone Age skulls with smashed-in faces has been found carefully separated from the rest of their skeletons. They appear to have been dug up several years after being buried with their bodies, separated, then reburied.

But how do you turn this into a story?

First, you need to ask yourself some questions –

Why would anyone dig up a dead body, break the skull and then re-bury the broken head somewhere else?

Could it be a ritual, a magic spell, an insult, did the dead rise by themselves?

Pick your reason, then come up with your characters. Who did this? What were they trying to achieve? Did they succeed? Suddenly you have a story.

Your stone age mystery idea …

When I saw this article I immediately thought of zombies. As we all know zombies can only be killed if you destroy the brain. I can only assume that stone age man fought a zombie apocalypse!

What if ...? And other great questions

It is easy to be inspired by the things that interest you, but what about the things that don't?

A few years ago, I was talking to my father-in-law about geocaching - not something that had previously piqued my interest. He was telling me that in geocaching you follow co-ordinates to the location of a box (the geocache), in which there will be a logbook and often a piece of 'treasure'. You are welcome to take the treasure as long as you replace it with something of equal or greater value.

As my father-in-law continued talking, I thought ...

WHAT IF YOU WERE GEO-CACHING AND, IN THE BOX, YOU FOUND A FINGER?

I got chills. I loved this.

So, my brain immediately went ...

Well okay, but why would you continue? Why would you replace it with something of equal or greater value (i.e. another finger, or other body part)?

Well, there are a few reasons I came up with for doing this - perhaps you are being coerced or blackmailed. Perhaps someone's life depends on it. Perhaps you are trying to solve a mystery. Perhaps there is (a lot of) money involved.

And that is how my award-winning, world-first, geocaching horror story, *Savage Island,* was born. It is a novel about a group of teenagers who enter a geo-caching competition to win £1m each, but the boxes contain some pretty awful stuff!

What if is the big question you need in your arsenal. When you need to come up with a story idea, even about something that doesn't interest you (for example for a school task), ask yourself **what if** …

What if aliens crashed the party?

What if your teacher was a vampire?

What if you found out that your real dad was a famous actor?

The ideas are endless …

Once you have your central 'what if', you need to sit your idea down in the centre of the room, tie it to a chair and ask it more questions.

So what?

How?

Why?

Who?

What next?

Soon you'll have a whole story planned out.

Other ways to come up with stories:

Characters

Think of any character: a brave fireman, a dedicated teacher, a shy student, a talented footballer, a committed detective – anything! Then think of the *worst thing* that could happen to them.

Your story is about the time this happened!

For example, what's the worst thing that could happen to a talented footballer? A broken ankle just before the big game, perhaps?

So, you now have a story about a footballer who breaks his ankle just before the big game. What does he do? Does he try and play anyway? Does he attempt to sabotage the game so that no-one can play until he's better? Does he end up discovering something important about himself that he'd never have known if he hadn't been stopped from playing that day?

Or perhaps you write a story about a shy student who is forced to dance in front of the whole school, or a woman who is terrified of heights, who ends up having to climb a tree to save her cat, or a detective who is forced to commit a crime …

Who is your character?

TOBY Tinker

What is their biggest fear?

he's frightened

How does it happen?

Time travels when he panics

What do they learn?

The Plot Game

If all else fails you should be able to come up with a story idea using this method.

Characteristics	Write a list of characteristics. These could be anything, make your own list! Here's mine … *Tall, funny, happy, red-haired, mean, generous, weak, strong, sporty, academic, ambitious, talkative, shy.*
Name	Then you pick names. Any names. *Ben. Claire. Rohan. Jake. Vaughan. Bridget.*
Wants to	Then you come up with a list of things that an individual might want to achieve. *Ace a test, become a singer, fly to the moon, become a millionaire, solve a crime, join the netball team, buy a gift, get a girlfriend, win a competition.*

Then you choose one thing from each category to create a character and situation, for example:

Talkative Ben wants to win a competition.

Sporty Rohan wants to ace a test.

But	Then there's the but, and that *must refer back to the characteristic.*

Talkative Ben wants to win a competition BUT the competition is to see who can remain silent for the longest and, for talkative Ben, this is absolute torture!

Sporty Rohan has to ace a test BUT he never studies, all he does is play basketball.

Can you see how you now have an idea for a story?

What challenges does *talkative Ben* face in trying to stay quiet? Is someone trying to sabotage him? Does he perhaps see something that he desperately needs to tell someone about (perhaps there is a crack in the roof, and it is about to fall in)? Does he win the competition, or not?

Why is acing the test so important to *sporty Rohan*? What challenges does he face? Does he find studying hard? Do his friends keep trying to make him play with them instead of study? Is there an important match that he is needed for on the day of the test? What does he choose in the end, sport or study? Perhaps he can find a way to combine the two and solve his problem?

Now *you* try, and don't forget to make your 'but' swing back to your original characteristic …

Characteristics	red Curly hair Curious Cheeky runny Wears odd socks Loyal always has one shoe untied always slightly crumpled appearance
Names	Toby Tinker
Wants to	
But	

By now you should have some really great story ideas.

The foundation bit

Building great characters

(Because no-one wants to read a book with rubbish ones)

Some of the story ideas that I talked about in the previous section, involved coming up with a character (a person from your story).

Well-written characters are perhaps the most important part of a good book. You might read a book with a terrible plot (storyline) if there is a character you really love, but you are unlikely to read a book with a good plot, but which has terrible characters who you can't stand.

When you read a book, the characters become your friends - no-one wants to hang out with people they don't like!

In other words, a good character might save a bad story, but a good story can't save a bad character.

If your plot is the skeleton of your story, the heart and soul is the character development.

(Bryony Pearce)

Characters are the way in which a reader will enter a story. As readers we imagine ourselves in the place of the character, living their adventure. It is their experiences, their emotions, their decisions which give us the route into the action.

If there are inconsistencies or bad description, the reader has no chance to get inside your protagonist (your hero), to sympathise, root for and care about them.

So, what makes a character a good character?

Good <u>characters</u> do not have to be good <u>people</u>.

Think about Artemis Fowl, Horrid Henry, Deadpool, Wolverine or John Constantine, great characters all, but are they good people?

Good characters *are* **memorable**, in both appearance and personality.

Good characters *are* **realistic**. We feel as if they are actual people that we could meet one day.

Good characters *are* **aspirational** – they're people that we want to *hang out with* or *be like*. Deadpool would be hilarious at a party, and who wouldn't want the powers of Voldemort, or Darth Vader, the style of Cruella de Vil, or the riches of the White Witch?

Good characters are **consistent**. If your character is meant to be brave, you shouldn't show them being cowardly. If your character is meant to be reckless, then you mustn't show them being careful.

Finally, good characters *are not* **perfect.**

Not only do perfect people simply not exist, but perfect people *kill stories*. They have no problems, nothing to learn and nowhere to grow. And, since perfect people never make mistakes, the reader will never worry about what is going to happen to them.

It would be like writing Superman and missing out the kryptonite. How boring would the Superman stories be if you knew that he would easily win every time?

What does your character look like?

Do you ever watch a film of a book you have read and think, *'that isn't how I pictured the character at all!'*? That is because the writer gave you a clear picture of the character in your mind, by describing them to you, and you brought them to life by filling in all the other parts yourself.

Readers want to be able to picture characters, so that they can see what is going on in the story.

Think about characters you know well, what makes them stand out to you:

Harry Potter has a scar on his forehead

Artemis Fowl always wears a suit.

Hester Shaw (Mortal Engines) has a dreadful scar across her face and only one eye.

When you are describing your character, you need to pick things that make them unique, so that they become memorable.

Never describe your character by hair and eye colour, *unless* you are going to give them something else special and unusual to distinguish them from others with the same features.

Oh, and while I'm here, *never* describe a character as having purple eyes (unless they're an alien). For a time, it seemed to be author shorthand for 'this character is unusual, interesting and gorgeous'. I cringe whenever I see it! Also, *no-one* has purple eyes.

Think of one of your friends who has purple eyes. … Go on … I'll wait.

Bad character description:

The girl had blonde hair and hazel eyes.

Am I describing Rebel Wilson, or Emma Roberts?

Better character description:

The girl bounced into the room, flicking her hair as she told a loud joke, laughing raucously before anyone else could get the punchline. She was all smiles, shoulder's-back voluptuousness and in-your-face confidence. Her skin was pale, her hands small and soft and it looked as if she'd tease you all night, then buy you a drink and make sure you got home safely.

Am I describing Rebel Wilson, or Emma Roberts?

Think hard about the characters you are building – do they have piercings? Tattoos? A particular style? Are they unusual in terms of weight or height (be careful of body shaming)? Do they always wear something unusual? Do they always have something in their mouth (gum, a toothpick, a lollipop etc.)? Do they always carry something, or play with something? Have they dyed their hair an unusual colour? Do they have an injury (do they walk with a limp, for example)?

Be careful with scars – don't use these as shorthand for 'this is a bad-guy'. It could be upsetting to your readers who might have scars of their own.

Here, as another example, is my description of Ayla from Phoenix Rising,

> *All the crewmen of the Banshee that Toby had seen so far were shaven and tattooed; men or women, it didn't seem to matter. This girl wore her hair long and loose and braids decorated with beads and feathers kept it from falling into her eyes. Beneath the decoration the strands were the colour of oil; black, which hinted of prisms of colour beneath.*

> *Despite his better judgement, Toby was unable to retreat. Instead, he balanced against the rise and fall of the ship and stared. The girl's eyes were shockingly green, algae on seawater. Her face was as tanned as Toby's, but her skin was not as salt-burned or work-rough. She hadn't the perfect face that Toby had seen in his dreams. Her cheeks were hollow, speaking of hunger and her nose had clearly been broken at least once.*

> *As he exhaled, his breath shivered in the air between them, and the girl put her hands on her hips to reveal black leather trousers and a tight waxed jerkin beneath her coat.*

Can you see how I have made it clear that she is different from everyone else? She is unusual because she *hasn't* had her head shaved and she has *no* tattoos (she is non-conformist). Instead, she has long hair, which she wears in braids filled with beads and feathers. Her hair is dark, but suggests colour underneath, this tells the reader that she is hiding her true self.

I wanted the reader to feel as if Ayla is a force of nature, so I link her to birds (which Toby loves) and to the sea (eyes the colour of algae on seawater). I also make it clear that she is flawed. She isn't 'the girl of Toby dreams', and immediately the reader dismisses this perfect dream girl as boring, because Ayla is fascinating.

She is hungry, she's a fighter (her broken nose), she's going to stand up to Toby and make him grow and change. Without saying a word, she's already challenged him and changed him (making him realise how boring his perfect dream girl was).

These two characters are going to challenge one another throughout the book. Toby represents order, serenity, technology. Ayla represents chaos, disruption and nature.

Look at the way that your favourite writers have described *their* characters. What words and phrases do they use, what attributes do they pick up on, how do they make their characters into real people by using description?

Writing Exercise

Look out of your window or go for a walk. Take a notebook. The next five people that you see, write descriptions of them into your notebook. Try and find what makes each person unique and interesting.

Why not keep this notebook? Keep filling it with descriptions of people who interest you. Then, when you are trying to come up with a new character, you will have a whole notebook filled with ideas you can use to describe them.

You could also look at this website, which gives some of the best character descriptions in science fiction and fantasy literature and also explains why each description works well:

http://io9.com/5823291/great-character-descriptions-from-science-fiction-and-fantasy-books

Strengths and Flaws

Now you know what your character looks like, you need to know *who they are*.

For my main characters I often write a note and put it by my laptop, this note tells me the character's **two main strengths** and **one weakness**, so that when I am writing scenes, I am always thinking about these, and how I can reveal them to the reader.

Ben (Savage Island): Brave and kind but too self-sacrificing.

Ivy (Raising Hell): Intelligent and strong, but thinks she can't rely on others.

Toby (Phoenix Rising): Calm and orderly, but too trusting.

Picking two strengths and a weakness is an easy way of giving your character the basics of a personality and keeping it consistent.

A useful list of strengths you can pick from

Bold / confident
Brave
Calm
Carefree
Careful
Clever
Competent
Confident
Constant
Creative
Decisive
Direct
Easy-going
Ethical
Experienced
Focused
Friendly
Funny
Generous
Good-humoured
Good leader
Good-tempered
Hard-working
Honest
Humble
Independent
Kind
Loyal

Mature
Merciful
Moderate
Modest
Mischievous
Non-judgemental
Patient
Polite
Practical
Profound
Proud (of others)
Quiet
Realistic
Refined
Relaxed
Rule-follower
Sensible
Serene / tranquil
Sincere
Stable
Strong
Tactful
Tolerant
Tractable
Unfazed / unruffled
Warm
Well-behaved
Worldly

Can you think of more strengths you can add to this list?

A useful list of flaws you can pick from

Absent minded	Greedy	Nosey
Aimless	Grumpy	Obsessive
Ambitious	Gullible	Paranoid
Anxious	Giddy / flighty	Perfectionist
Arrogant	Humourless	Predictable
Blunt / insensitive	Hypocritical	Proud
Brazen / cheeky	Ignorant	Rebellious
Callous / unfeeling	Impatient	Reckless
Childish / immature	Incompetent	Relentless
Clumsy	Indecisive	Rude
Cowardly / Spineless	Intolerant	Sceptical
Confident	Judgemental	Selfish
Dependent	Know it all	Shallow
Dishonest	Lazy	Shy
Disloyal	Loudmouthed	Smart-alec
Egotistical / Boastful	Manipulative	Spoiled
Emotional	Mean	Stubborn
Envious / jealous	Meddlesome	Superstitious
Fickle / changeable	Merciless	Tactless
Fastidious / finicky	Moody	Vain
Flirty	Naïve	Weak-willed
Frail / weak	Naughty	Zealous / fanatical

Can you think of any more flaws you could add to this list?

More on interesting flaws

We already know that no-one wants to read about Mister Perfect, living his perfect life! This is why gossip columns are so popular - as a species, we like to read about the flaws of people who present a perfect face to the world. Flaws are simply more interesting than strengths.

Professional writers usually give their heroes flaws to overcome, which often drives the problems they face in their stories.

Percy Jackson is too loyal – he will risk everything for his friends.

Harry Potter is too proud – he thinks he has to do everything alone - he doesn't trust anyone else to do the right thing.

Katniss Everdeen is too self-sacrificing – she always puts others ahead of herself, even when that isn't the best move.

In writing there are three kinds of flaw:

A **minor flaw** is an imperfection which makes the character memorable and individual but doesn't affect the story.

For example, your character might be a teacher who is absent-minded so always forgets his glasses and squints all the time.

A **major flaw** is more noticeable and actually causes real problems for the individual.

For example, your character might be a gambler, who cannot walk past any game without placing a bet.

A **fatal flaw** causes a character's downfall or even death.

For example, if your character was a firefighter, her fatal flaw might be recklessness, which leads her to run into a fire before the building is made safe, causing her to be killed.

If you've done Shakespeare at school you will know about the fatal flaw, the defect inside each of his tragic characters that ultimately results in their downfall.

Romeo is impulsive - he rushes into every decision, never thinking about consequences.

Hamlet is indecisive - the opposite of Romeo, he can never commit to a course of action.

Macbeth is ambitious and paranoid – he wants to be king, and he'll do anything to achieve his goal, but he thinks that everyone else is as ambitious as he is.

King Lear is proud – he throws out his youngest daughter (the only one who truly loves him) because she won't display her love as a trophy for him to gloat over.

Othello is jealous – he too easily believes that his young wife is betraying him.

If you are writing a heroic character (the protagonist), I would g. them only minor or major flaws. Your antagonist (bad guy) character could have a fatal flaw, which enables the protagonist to defeat them.

What might your character be:

Strength	
Strength	
Flaw	

Building a realistic personality

Of course, there is more to building a character than just giving them two strengths and a flaw. Great characters have *fully rounded* personalities.

One way to make your characters into real people is to base them on real personality types. People tend to fall into four different personality types (more or less).

These personality types are laid out below.

Processor:	Enthusiast:
Formal, quiet, logical, thorough. Likes time to think. Hates to be rushed or interrupted. Bases decisions on facts. When stressed they avoid.	Sociable, energetic, enthusiastic, flexible, spontaneous. Easily bored. Opinionated, but welcomes other views. Hates facts and routine. When stressed they attack.
Controller:	Supporter:
Business-like. Wants to get things done and likes to be in charge. Hates indecision and inefficiency. Hates to lose control. Bases decisions on facts. When stressed they demand.	Friendly, informal; avoids confrontation. Thinks of others first. Hates insensitivity. Bases decisions on feelings. Likes time to make decisions. Hates too many facts. When stressed they give up.

Can you recognise any of your friends or family members in these groups? What about you, what personality type are you?

Now would be a good time to decide which personality type your character is going to be!

Each of these different personality types behaves in a different, consistent way.

Processor: Pace: Measured, systematic Voice: Quiet, monotone Posture: Formal, stiff Gestures: Small, few Eye Contact: Reflective, steady Face: Fixed, inexpressive	Enthusiast: Pace: Fast Voice: Loud, fast, dynamics Posture: Relaxed, open Gestures: Large, frequent Eye Contact: Intense, but infrequent Face: Very animated.
Controller: Pace: Fast, decisive Voice: Clipped, monotone Posture: Formal, forward Gestures: Small, precise Eye Contact: Intense, direct Face: Fixed, immobile	Supporter: Pace: Slow, easy Voice: Soft, dynamics, Posture: Relaxed, informal Gestures: Large, but few Eye Contact: Warm, friendly Face: Open, animated

Now, when you are describing your character, you know how to make them act, how they will walk, speak, sit, gesture, what facial expressions they might use.

Using this system is helpful, because if you make your protagonist an *Enthusiast*, for example, you know that if you write them as sociable, energetic, spontaneous, flexible, hating routine, getting bored easily and showing that they will fight back when attacked, and make them loud, animated and fast moving, readers will think ...

'Hey, that's just like my friend, I like this person!'

Backstory

So now you know how to describe your character, to give your character two strengths and a flaw and to select a personality type for your character.

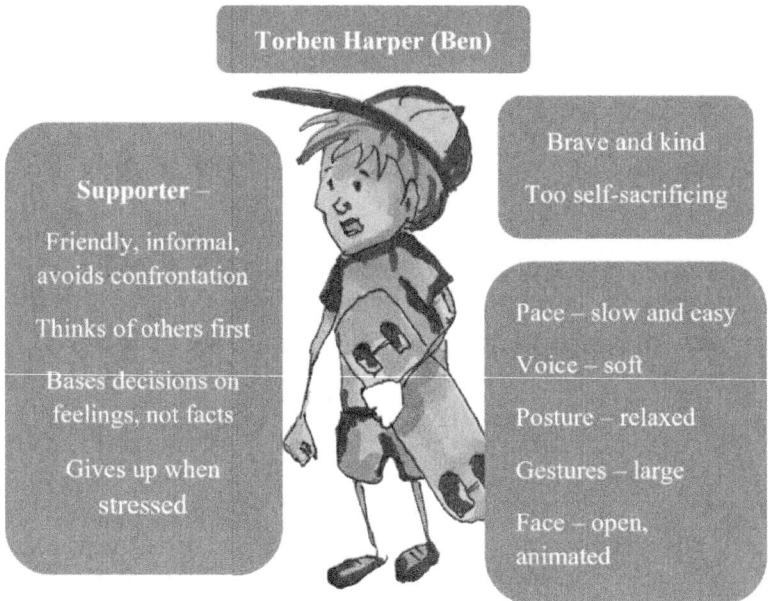

Torben Harper (Ben)

Supporter –

Friendly, informal, avoids confrontation

Thinks of others first

Bases decisions on feelings, not facts

Gives up when stressed

Brave and kind

Too self-sacrificing

Pace – slow and easy

Voice – soft

Posture – relaxed

Gestures – large

Face – open, animated

What I don't have yet is a history, or backstory for the character.

The information I have on Ben is great, but I haven't really got to *know* him - why does he make the decisions he does? Why is he too self-sacrificing and always think of others first?

This is where a pen picture comes in.

A pen picture is a questionnaire you fill in, to help you get to know your character. Here is a pen picture for you to fill in for your characters:

Full name	Charlotte Bronte
What do they look like? Three characteristics	
What are their strengths?	
What is their flaw?	
What is their favourite food and why?	
What do they like to wear and why?	
What is their favourite piece of music and why?	
What is their favourite place and why?	
What do they most like to do and why?	
What are their main responsibilities?	
What do they want to be when they grow up / do with their life?	
What do they sound like (accent, verbal expressions, tone)?	
What is their biggest secret?	
What do they want to change about themselves?	
Who is their hero?	
What is their biggest fear?	
What is the worst thing that could happen to them?	

Here is an example of a pen picture I wrote for Ben Harper, the protagonist in my novel, *Savage Island*.

Full name: *Torben Harper (Ben)*

What does he look like? *Ben has ginger hair, which he keeps short, so that it doesn't curl too much, he has strong leg and core muscles because he enjoys skateboarding and he has a strong, wide jaw.*

What is his favourite food and why? *Ben loves to eat chips (secretly), because his mother is always putting him and his brother on the Atkins diet and he loves carbs.*

What is his favourite item of clothing, film, piece of music and place? Why? *Ben's favourite film is The Martian, partly because he feels so out of place in his own family, and partly because it is about engineering and survival and he is really interested in engineering.*

He loves to wear his skateboarding shorts and his dad's old Tony Hawk t-shirt, because he loves skateboarding, it's something he is really good at, and he has great memories of his dad teaching him the basics.

He loves old jazz singers, like Nina Simone, because that is what Lizzie listens to and it reminds him of her.

His favourite place is Lizzie's bedroom, where he always feels safe and loved and where they used to play Zelda on the Nintendo.

What does he most like to do? *Ben loves to skateboard and spend time with Lizzie.*

What are his main responsibilities: *Ben has to look after his brother, Will, who isn't quite ... normal.*

What does he want to do with his life? *Ben wants to go to Cardiff university to study engineering, because he wants to build bridges, he has become fascinated with the architecture he has seen while skateboarding. He also wants to spend the rest of his life with Lizzie, he can't imagine being without her. They've been friends since the first day of school.*

What does he sound like (accent, verbal expressions, tone)? *Ben has a South Midlands accent, he uses a lot of skateboarding terms.*

What does he most like about himself? *Ben is proud of his skills on the skateboard and he likes who he is when he is with Lizzie (braver, more heroic).*

What does he want to change about themselves? *Ben has low self-esteem due to the way his brother and his mum treat him and because his father left the family. He believes that if he had been better at keeping his brother calm, his father would have stayed. He wishes he were more self-confident.*

Who is his hero? Why? *His father is his hero, he loved him a lot, and although he misses him, he is secretly impressed that he was brave enough to leave his abusive wife (Ben's mother). He asked Ben to go with him, but Ben knew he had to stay and look after his younger brother.*

What is his biggest fear? Why? *Ben is terrified of something happening with Will on his watch. He has been raised to look after his brother and if something happens, then he'll be a failure.*

What is the worst thing that could happen to them? *Losing his brother Will, or someone being hurt, and it being his fault.*

What are his two or three best attributes? *Ben is kind and brave.*

What is his flaw? *Ben is too self-sacrificing. All of his focus is on Will, and he doesn't know himself very well.*

Can you see how writing the reasons for Ben's behaviours, his backstory, helps me to know him better?

And, of course, this pen picture tells me what Ben's story is going to be. He has been raised as his brother's keeper and his biggest fear is failing in that role, of something happening to his brother. In *Savage Island*, therefore, something is going to happen to Ben's brother, Will, and Ben's ability to protect him will be tested to its limit.

Other characters

When you are writing a story there will be more than one character. This where things get *really* fun!

Make characters whose personalities, needs and wants, *conflict* with those of your main character.

For example, in *Savage Island*, what drives Ben is looking after his brother, but what drives his brother, Will, is the desire to get out from under his brother's watchful eye.

Give character's opposing personalities. If your hero is an Enthusiast, make your antagonist (your bad guy) a Controller.

If your main character likes to help people, create someone else who doesn't want to be helped.

If your main character likes things calm and orderly, create a whirlwind of a character who destroys everything in their path.

This creates conflict and problems, and this makes a good story!

Character arc

During the course of your story, your character will likely change as a person.

Think about *Star Wars: A New Hope*. When we first meet Han Solo, he is a loner, a mercenary, who only does things that help Han Solo. By the end of the film, he has discovered the value of friendship and self-sacrifice.

Think about Hermione in *Harry Potter*, another loner but this time one who values rules and learning above all, who learns that some things are more important than books and that sometimes rules are made to be broken!

Or Tiffany Aching (*The Wee Free Men*) who learns to love her family, even though she's the odd one out.

While you are planning your story, think about who your character is at the beginning and who they are going to be at the end – What will they learn? How will they change? What is going to change them?

Introducing your character

Pat the dog

Now you've created the most excellent character possible, you want the reader to love them. The faster they fall in love with your character, the more likely they are to want to read your story.

There are two ways to introduce a character which should make the reader fall immediately in love with them.

The first is called *pat the dog*.

Basically, what this means is you show your character *doing something nice*: patting a dog, helping an old lady cross the road, carrying heavy shopping, doing the laundry to help Mum. Anything nice at all.

But this nice thing *must be part of their normal life* and *must not be out of character*.

So, in *Savage Island*, before the end of page one, Ben opens a six-pack of cola and hands them out to his friends.

> *I leaned my skateboard against the doorway, took a coke from the six-pack Grady handed me from his bag and passed the rest around.*

In the first chapter of *Raising Hell*, Ivy is trying to save younger teenagers from 'witchcraft'.

> *I held her eyes; establish dominance, that was the first thing. Make her believe she had to do as I said, even though I was only three or four years older.*

My favourite example from film is the opening scene of *Despicable Me*.

https://youtu.be/bx7PdmKIC3U

This opening shows the main character, Gru, strolling through the park, when he sees a boy drop his ice-cream and start to cry. Quickly he pulls out a balloon and makes an animal for him. The boy takes it, and cuddles it, he is now all smiles. Immediately the viewer thinks –

> *'What a nice person this Gru is. I like him. I want to watch his story.'*

Gru is a villain, however, so this would be out of character for him and would not work, if left as is. So, he takes a pin, bursts the balloon and walks away smiling, as the boy stands there frozen in shock. This is a hilarious moment which also shows us Gru's villainous nature.

But … it's, very cleverly, too late. The viewer has already had that moment, of *I like him, I will watch his story*, we are *invested* and, not only that, but we don't believe that Gru is a real villain. We spend the rest of the story waiting for that good guy we glimpsed at the beginning to turn up again. And, of course, he does.

Pat the dog is an incredibly effective way of making your reader invest in your character, whether they be good or bad.

Kill the parents

The other way of introducing a character who the reader will love is **undeserved suffering**, which I call *kill the parents.*

Oh, Daddy!

Would you like a drink?

Kill the parents actually means showing your main character *suffering through no fault of their own.*

In other words, you could kill off their parents …

Orphan, Harry Potter is raised by his cruel aunt and uncle and made to live in a cupboard.

Oliver Twist is raised in an orphanage.

Ivy Mann (*Raising Hell*) lives alone because her parents walked out on her.

Toby (*Phoenix Rising*) has no mother and isn't allowed to ever leave the pirate ship.

However, you don't have to literally kill off the parents in order to create a character who is suffering undeservedly. There are other ways a character can be suffering.

> August (*Wonder*) has a rare facial abnormality.

> Katniss Everdeen (*Hunger Games*) lives under the rule of a cruel and capricious authoritarian government.

> Ben Harper (*Savage Island*) isn't allowed a life of his own, he has to give up his dreams to look after his brother.

> Laurence Roach (*Fifteen days without a head*) has an alcoholic mother and has been parentified.

> Taylor Oh (*The Weight of Souls*) sees dead people but everyone thinks she's crazy.

That said, having your character lose their parents is probably the most common and effective trope in literature. This is partly because it makes the poor hero suffer undeservedly, but it is also because it removes the authority figures on which they might otherwise rely.

There is a reason that most MG / YA books remove adult authority figures early on, whether by removing the characters from the parental sphere physically (the characters in *Savage Island* go off to a literal island to take part in a competition, the children in *Peter Pan* go to Neverland, the boys in *Lord of the Flies* are stranded on a deserted island), by making them generally useless or clueless (In *Mansfield Park* the mother is more interested in her dog than her children, in *The Wee Free Men*, Tiffany Aching's parents are too preoccupied to notice what she is doing), by making the parent the villain, that the children must escape (*Matilda*, *The Shining*, *The*

Northern Lights), or by killing off the parent / guardian / mentor character (in *The Weight of Souls*, the woman who would have believed Taylor - her mother, who suffered from the same curse - has died, in *Harry Potter,* Dumbledore has to die once Harry has learned all he needs to know from him).

This is because the hero of the story needs to be proactive, to make their own decisions, to find their own path.

No-one wants to read about a main character who is going on an adventure because their dad told them to, or who is just dragged through the story by their mum.

Dialogue and Voice

(Because great characters speak)

You may be surprised to hear that some writers are scared of dialogue, but if you can master it the skill will make your writing so much better.

The fact is, humans are social. We have social brains, social hormones and social cognition. Connecting with others increases our happiness. Put two strangers in a room and it is likely that eventually they will speak to one another (especially of one of those strangers is me!).

A piece of writing that includes characters, but not speech, feels forced and unnatural.

Yes, dialogue *is* important. It gives a change of pace and tone (and changing pace and tone is essential to keeping readers interested – more on that later), it can add conflict (for example via an argument), it can move the story on, and, through dialogue, you can reveal information about a character easily and naturally.

Dialogue, for example can show us …

Where someone is from -

'That's a lovely wee kitten!'

'This is nothing like the weather back home in Manchester.'

Social status -

'The butler is late with the tea.'

'Awright, pet, don't get yer knickers in a twist!'

Attitudes, opinions and feelings -

'Oh, I do love the beach!'

Character appearances -

'All right, gingernut?'

'Hey, is that a new tattoo?'

Back story -

'Where've you been then?'

Exposition

'Now, listen … this is how we're going to defeat the evil wizard …'

Time / place / weather

'It's freezing out.'

'It's only half past two.'

'Careful, it's getting dark.'

Good dialogue *keeps the story or novel going, reveals something important* about the characters, is *believable* and interests the reader because it *contains tension or suspense.*

In order to *keep the story going*, dialogue must do one of these:

Provide new information about the conflict,

'Of course, it wasn't me,' he smiled. 'But I did arrange to have it done.'

Reveal new obstacles between the Main Character (MC) and their goal,

Grady was frowning at the phone. 'This can't be right!' He shook it, then switched it off and on again. 'This thing's meant to work at the North Pole.'

'What's the matter?' Carmen asked.

'It's got one-hundred-percent global coverage!' Grady was yelling at the phone now. 'It's impossible. Iridium satellites are low-earth orbit. There's literally no way I could have no reception.'

'No GPS?' Lizzie frowned.

'Nothing! There's something weird going on here!'

Create a dynamic between characters that furthers the theme,

'Do you think we can make it?' My binoculars dangled from my numb fingers.

Will nodded. 'No matter what, you'll get us out of here, that's what you do.'

'What I do?'

'You think I haven't noticed – you've always looked after me. You won't let anything happen.'

Introduce a pivotal moment in the plot,

'That's a human tooth,' Grady said weakly. 'It's got a filling!'

Remind us of goals,

'I don't know what's going on here,' Lizzie said. 'But there will be someone at checkpoint seven, there has to be. We just have to be strong for one more day.' She swallowed. 'Twenty-four hours. Less.'

Accelerate emotion to make the situation more urgent.

'Why didn't you tell me your dad's sick?'

(Quotes from Savage Island)

You can also use dialogue to tell your story (screenwriters do it all the time) and this can be very effective indeed.

Which of these examples works better?

Example 1	Example 2
Gill staggered into the room, her face was pale, and blood ran from a cut on her forehead. They all stared at her in horror as they realised that he was on his way.	*"He's coming," Gill cried. She staggered into the room, holding a hand to her bleeding forehead. "We've got to run!"*

Personally, I think the version where Gill uses dialogue to tell her friends that 'he' is coming is more effective. It has more emotional impact, is faster-paced and creates more tension.

Look at this piece of writing, which tells a story using dialogue.

Dylan and Max are going to break into the headmaster's office:

> *"Go on then," Max gave Dylan a shove. "You go first."*
>
> *"It was your flippin' idea." Dylan twisted out of the way.*
>
> *"It's your phone." Max frowned. "I thought you wanted it back."*
>
> *"Yeah, but if I get in trouble again, Mum'll 'ave me sent to Dad's. You get started an I'll keep watch."*
>
> *Max looked up and down the corridor. "There's no-one coming. Mr Davis is still running detention."*
>
> *"Nothing stopping you then, is there?"*
>
> *"Fine." Max sighed and bent to the doorknob. "You think Cara's right about her hairgrip working on the lock?"*
>
> *Dylan turned to look at him. "I 'ope so."*
>
> *"What do you boys think you're doing?"*

What has happened in this scene?

Are Max and Dylan the same / different? In what ways and how can we tell?

Who has turned up at the end? How can you tell?

Do be careful when using dialogue to tell the reader what is going on (exposition). Characters shouldn't tell each other things that they already know.

Bad dialogue:

'Remember that time we made your brother eat worms in the park and our mums grounded us and that's how we became best friends?'

'Yeah, totally! And now we're in year six and have to dissect worms for our science project, which is due tomorrow.'

These boys know how they became best friends, that they're in year six and that the science project is due without talking about it. So, it's very clear to the reader that they're not talking to each other: they're really talking <u>to the reader</u>. If I wanted to convey the same information, using dialogue, I might write the following:

'Ewww, this worm is gross! I don't want to cut it open.'

'Well, Mrs Simpson wants this handed in tomorrow, so tough! Anyway, remember when we made your brother eat a whole handful? That was gross!'

'OMG, Mum totally flipped!'

'Worm-buddies forever!'

'I still don't want to cut this one up.'

'Boys you are in year six now, so stop acting like pre-schoolers and do your work!'

Good dialogue also shows mood.

If you choose strong words in your dialogue, you can make it more emotional and effective, which means you don't have to write 'he said angrily', 'she sighed', 'he said sadly' etc.

Let what your characters are saying, show the reader how they are feeling.

"I freakin' hate this stupid house!"

How do you think this character is feeling?

"I just thought ... you might ... never mind."

How do you think this character is feeling?

Pick the strongest verbs and adjectives that you can, to add detailed images that your reader can see in their minds such as *Snatched, choked, grinned, threw, pinched, screamed, etc.*

"I choked her, don't you understand? I pinched her wallet, then I choked her dead."

Presenting dialogue correctly

One thing you will need to do when writing dialogue is present it correctly. These are the rules for correctly laying out your dialogue.

1. Begin on a **new line for each new speaker**.

   'You aren't supposed to pick wildflowers, you know?' Grady said.

   'We're on holiday, Grady! Relax.'

2. Have double or single **quotation marks around the words** (be consistent with which you choose). Either is fine, but publishers recently have been asking for me to use single quotation marks, so this seems to be the more modern choice.

3. **End the dialogue line with a comma if you're adding a tag** (he said), **a full stop if you're adding an action**.

   'We could've died!' Carmen grabbed Grady and placed a wet kiss on his cheek. 'You saved us, Grady.' She wrapped her arm around Will. 'And you, Will.'

   'This wasn't a good start,' Grady said.

   I snorted a laugh and suddenly we were all giggling.

4. **Punctuation goes *inside* the quotation marks**.

   'Are you OK?' Grady called.

   I nodded, then looked up. 'Our rucksacks!'

5. Use **commas before names in dialogue**.

> *'Will's your brother, Ben. Why would you say that about him?'*

6. **Don't use double punctuation marks** - go with the stronger / more important piece of punctuation. If your character is asking a question, use a question mark. If they're shouting, or exclaiming, use a single exclamation mark.

   Interrobangs are a recently acceptable piece of punctuation (?!), but honestly, I find them lazy, hysterical and unprofessional looking. It's up to you if you want to use them of course, I personally don't.

7. Do use **ellipses** (…) to show hesitation and a **dash** (-) to show an interruption.

   > *'What do you think of the -'*
   > *'Don't ask, sweetheart, just … don't ask.'*

8. The **three-sentence rule**. This rule is something that will make your dialogue effective and realistic. Basically, what is means is that you should give no character more than three uninterrupted sentences at once. People don't tend to speechify, without interruption, unless they are literally giving a speech. So, if a character has a lot to say, break their dialogue up every three sentences or so with a bit of action, an interruption, a question, a sound, anything. You'll be amazed at how much more naturally the speech flows.

Speech without interruptions:

*'That assessment form with all the questions on it -
Gold was looking for kids who fit his criteria. The
competition wouldn't be any good if there weren't
people on the island with psychopathic personalities,
would it? I mean, look how fast the teams out there
started cutting each other up! It's the only reason we
got into the lottery in the first place – isn't it, Will?'*

Adding realistic breaks:

*'That assessment form with all the questions on it -
Gold was looking for kids who fit his criteria.' I
rubbed my eyes and flinched as my palm caught my
swollen nose. 'The competition wouldn't be any good
if there weren't people on the island with
psychopathic personalities, would it? I mean, look
how fast the teams out there started cutting each
other up!'*

Lizzie stared. 'You're telling me that one of us ...'

*'It's the only reason we got into the lottery in the first
place.' I closed my arms around my stomach and
looked at my brother. 'Isn't it, Will?'*

Are these right or wrong?

Writing Exercise	Is this right or wrong?
"There isn't any milk left"!	Wrong
"Why can't we go today?"	right
"look over there!" Mark cried.	
"Why, if it isn't little Davy". He shook his head.	
'Hi Yihuan do you want to go to the park?'	
'Take your hands off me,' he said.	
'Don't touch that please.' She picked up the hot kettle and moved it across the counter.	

Tags

A **dialogue tag** is the bit you add onto the end of the piece of dialogue which tells the reader *who is speaking*.

Examples of dialogue tags:

'Fetch me that banana,' he said.   Dialogue tag

'Go away,' she whispered.   Dialogue tag

An **action tag** is the bit you add onto the end of the piece of dialogue which tells the reader *what the speaker is doing*.

Examples of action tags:

'Don't do that, please.' He frowned.   Action tag

'There's a car coming!' She pulled the little boy onto the pavement.   Action tag

In total, there are three ways of tagging dialogue.

1. You can write 'he said / she said'.
2. You can use synonyms for said, such as opined, murmured, shouted, yelled, puzzled, exclaimed etc.
3. You can use action tags.

The key with using dialogue tags, however, is to *keep them unobtrusive*, the dialogue itself is the most important thing in the text.

If it is obvious who is speaking, you can even avoid using a tag at all.

'Nikita, can you take the rubbish out?' Mum called.

'Oh, Mum, do I have to?'

However, you may be surprised to discover that it is absolutely fine to use the dialogue tags he said / she said. These are unobtrusive words. The brain essentially skips over them, allowing the reader to focus on the dialogue itself.

If you want to add a little oomph to 'he said' you could add an adverb (but don't do this too often, the reader should be able to identify how the character is speaking by what he says and what he is doing while he says it).

'You'll find out,' he said, darkly.

You can vary the rhythm of your writing and make dialogue feel more interesting by changing the place in which you write your dialogue tag.

'Nikita,' Mum called, 'can you take the rubbish out?'

So, he said / she said is fine. However, using lots of synonyms for said is not.

If you use a lot of synonyms for said, the reader's attention is suddenly taken by the tag, not the dialogue. You are saying to the reader ...

'Hey, look at my big vocabulary!'

or even

'Look at me - I own a thesaurus!'

72

When what you are meant to be saying is …

'Don't look at what <u>I</u> am saying, look at what <u>my character</u> is saying.'

Read this piece of dialogue and write down what you think of it –

'Are you sure want to keep walking?' I questioned.

'I'm sure,' Lizzie insisted. 'I'm excited to get to the second checkpoint,' she exclaimed. 'Aren't you?' she asked.

'Can you see any other teams?' I puzzled.

'I can't see anyone,' she opined.

'But there's the river,' I bellowed.

'And we're going to have to ford that, aren't we?' Lizzie groaned.

I'll give you a clue, it's TERRIBLE WRITING. It's distracting, clunky and confusing.

Now try reading it without those awful synonyms!

'Are you sure want to keep walking?'

'I'm sure,' Lizzie said. 'I'm excited to get to the second checkpoint, aren't you?'

'Can you see any other teams?' I asked.

'I can't see anyone.'

'But there's the river,' I said.

'And we're going to have to ford that, aren't we?' Lizzie said.

Can you see how it flows much more naturally? Do you agree now that it is better to use said than puzzled, opined, groaned, sighed etc.?

There are a few exceptions to this rule.

Sometimes it is appropriate to show the reader the volume of speech, so I've been known to use whispered, murmured, shouted or yelled when writing dialogue.

If it is cleaner to use *said* in your writing than e.g. *expectorated*, then what about action tags? Well, this is where you can make your writing seem really professional.

An **action tag** is where you show the reader what the character is doing. It can come before or after the dialogue

'I hate chips!' Marcus shoved the plate away.

Abby grinned. 'I love going to the park!'

Shehnaz reached into the back of the cupboard. Her shoulders slumped. 'There aren't any biscuits left.'

Now read the same piece of dialogue I used above, but as it was *published.*

'Are you sure you want to keep walking?' I helped Lizzie over a rotting trunk.

'I'm sure.' She forced a smile. 'I'm excited to get to the second checkpoint, aren't you?'

*'Absolutely. It's just that I know how much you're hurting –
remember last year?'*

*I'd wiped out doing a fifty-fifty grind on my skateboard and
landed hard, with my wrist twisted under me.*

*'Lucky you didn't break your arm that time.' Lizzie grinned,
then flinched and paled as she put too much weight on her ankle.*

*Finally, we stepped into the open. The wind ruffled my hair
gently, as though it was considering turning in for the night.*

*'Can you see any other teams?' I whispered as if leaving the
trees meant we had to drop our voices.*

*She put the binoculars to her eyes. 'I can't see anyone.' The
river was directly ahead. She sighed. 'We're going to have to forge
that, aren't we?'*

Can you see how I have avoided using dialogue tags as much as
possible (I only use one – *I whispered*), and instead used action tags,
which *show* the reader what the characters are doing.

Professional writers use a mixture of action tags, he said / she said
and *a few* synonyms for said, which are as uncomplicated as possible.

Writing exercise
Why not try rewriting some of your own dialogue? Simplify all your dialogue tags (either remove them altogether or use he / she said) and break up your dialogue with action tags. Think about your characters, where are they? How are they reacting to one another and the world around them? What are they doing?

Accents and Dialect

One of the things that dialogue can do is show the reader where someone is from.

You can use accents to suggest a background for the reader and accents are one great way of distinguishing otherwise similar characters from one another.

'All right, me luvver, I'll be up dreckly.' (Devon)

'D'you want a barm cake with your loaf?' (Cheshire)

'Howay man, how's the crack?' (Northumberland)

'Come on, our kid, quit gawping and let's get the bus.' (Birmingham)

'G'wed girl! We're made up, she won 'er match!' (Liverpool)

'Dinnae teach yer granny tae suck eggs!' (Scotland)

'What beautiful weather we are having.' (Received Pronunciation)

I could go on forever with these, Irish, Welsh, Cornish, Cockney ... the list goes on.

For a great video on British accents, do watch this one, which will educate you on the key features of twenty British accents.

https://m.youtube.com/watch?v=u_BDG9JtGw8

However, do not go over the top with dialect words or accents. If you do, you could make your dialogue incomprehensible, unintentionally comical, or even offensive.

> *Jist oncest, Jist oncest. I wid like tae be able talk tae you withoot feelin... like I've jist gargled wie *Preparation X!*
> *(Rab C Nesbitt)*

The above quote is from Rab C Nesbitt and part of the humour was that he was *meant to be* difficult to understand (outside of Glasgow). The series was in fact shown in the US with subtitles!

If you want to show that your character has an accent, then the trick is, less is more. If your character is from Scotland, for example, then add a couple of familiar Scottish words ('wee' or 'tae' perhaps) and leave the rest – most readers will be able to fill in the Scottish accent in their imaginations, once they know that they are meant to be doing this.

To show that your character is uneducated, for example, then using non-standard grammar or phrases (for example, ain't) will be enough to establish their voice – you don't need to start knocking letters off every word.

Swearing and slang

If you've turned to this chapter because you think I've written a list of swear words for you to memorise, then I'm afraid you're going to be disappointed. I'm sure you know a few, and I don't need your parents knocking on my door because I've taught you a whole bunch more!

The thing with swearing in literature, especially literature for young people, is that it really isn't necessary most of the time.

You can write -

'Watch out the beast is coming!'

Roslyn cursed. 'Everybody … run!'

Or just

'Watch out the beast is coming!'

Roslyn leaped to her feet. 'Everybody … run!'

Swearing is a good short-cut to show strong emotion, and yes, it does have its place, but it isn't the only way and most of the time you can do without it.

If you are writing something that you think really requires a swear word, treat it like shock-and-awe weaponry and only use it once. A single swear word to show that the character has reached their absolute emotional limit can be effective, but *not* if you've already sprinkled in a whole handful already.

Something else you could do is make up your own swear words. If you're writing about a different place and time, or setting your story in another world, or setting it among a particular group of people (e.g. close friends) who's to say that they wouldn't have their own vocabulary, including swear words?

There are lots of great examples in literature or on TV.

Smeg (*Red Dwarf*)

Frak (*Battlestar Galactica*)

Frell (*Farscape*)

Gorram (*Firefly*)

Shazbot (*Mork and Mindy*)

Ashes (*Phoenix Rising*)

(There you go, I did give you a list, after all).

Slang is another great way to show where a character is from and indicate their social class. However, do be careful with slang. There are problems with using real slang in literature, related to the fact that language is ever-evolving and that slang evolves faster than anything else:

Problem 1. **Slang dates.**

When I wrote my first novel, *Angel's Fury*, I included an American character, named Max. I had a friend from New-York, so I asked her for some common US slang that I could sprinkle into Max's speech. She told me that everyone over there used the word '*rad*'. Brilliant, I thought, and so Max uses the word *rad* whenever he sees something that he thinks is cool. Once the book was published, I received numerous messages from American teenagers mocking Max (and me!). Apparently '*rad*' is something that only incredibly uncool over-thirties say. Some said it was the equivalent of having my UK teens saying 'cor blimey' all the time. Which certainly made me cringe. And that made sense, as my friend was, indeed, over thirty! Poor Max ...

Problem 2. **Slang words can mean different things in different places -**

When I was young, we had a word: 'flob'. Where I came from this meant 'spit'. I went to university and one of my friends turned around and said,

> '*I'm off to flob in the TV room!*'

I was HORRIFIED. How disgusting!

Later I discovered that where she was from (Birmingham), the word 'flob' actually meant 'relax'. Luckily, our friendship survived the misunderstanding. But you don't want your readers being similarly confused about your meanings if you use slang.

Problem 3: **Readers might not know what the slang word means at all** –

What if I wrote the following dialogue:

'I came first in the race.'

'Shub!'

What do you think I mean? You could guess from context. Perhaps you think that 'shub' means congratulations?

Actually 'shub' was a very particular piece of slang from my time at university which essentially meant 'yeah, right!' (as in – *I don't believe you*).

The only sensible way to use slang in your writing is to make up your own. This can add to the unique voice of your character and make them memorable, and it can give a sense of shared history to a group.

Distinct speech patterns

You should be able to pull a piece of dialogue out of your writing and your reader be easily able to tell who is speaking. Make sure your characters sound different. If you take out your tags, is it still clear who said what?

When giving your characters their unique voices, think about:

- **How old they are -** a 13-year-old will speak differently to a 70-year-old.
- **What gender they are** – different genders often use different vocabulary.
- **Their social background -** does your character use down-to-earth words or "posh" ones?
- **Their level of education**– does your character have a wide or limited vocabulary?
- **Where they are from** – Do they have an accent, or use regional slang?
- **Their catch-phrases -** Does your character have any common phrases ('for sure!', 'awesome' etc.)?
- **Verbosity** – Does your character babble, or prefer to remain quiet?
- **Their interests** – Characters with different interests will see the world differently. For example, someone who loves art might see colours and shapes first when looking at something, someone who loves engineering might see how something is made, someone who loves dance might see how something moves and so on.

- **Their job** – Different jobs might give your characters different vocabularies.
- **Their religion** – If a character is particularly religious, this might impact on what they say and how they say it.

Writing exercise	
Try taking each of the below characters and writing a single line of dialogue that is recognisably from that character (and only that character). Try reading your examples out to family members to see if they can guess which character said what.	
Teacher	
Cleaner	
Pensioner	
Soldier	
Nurse	
Pre-schooler	
Journalist	
Scientist	
Rich woman	
Film director	
Actress	
Struggling artist	
Comic book nerd	
Farmer	
Estate agent	
Bus driver	
Hippy	
Pilot	

Building a believable world

Now you have your characters, they need a world to inhabit. I've mentioned how important it is to describe your characters well, but it is also essential to show the reader *where they are*. The more clearly that we can picture a scene, the more we enjoy reading a story (remember that film in your head?).

World building is about creating a sense of place. Your character will need to interact with the world around them and the world in which your character lives may affect what happens to them in your story.

You could be writing about a character who lives in Pompeii – the volcano erupting will likely be a big part of the narrative.

You could write a story about a character who lives in a desert, or under the sea. How they deal with the challenges of that inhospitable landscape will inform the development of their character.

But, even if you aren't writing about a different time and place, your characters will need to interact with their world - driving a car, making a cup of tea, taking a walk, these are all the kinds of things that will make your story feel real.

If you are writing a contemporary story, set in a familiar modern landscape you probably won't need to do a lot of world-building. Don't take the modern world for granted though, it is usually best to set a contemporary story somewhere you know.

I recently read an online thread where an American author wanted to be given a few Britishisms because they were writing a book set in the UK (somewhere they had never been) and wanted to sprinkle a few details that would make it seem real. My advice was to set the book in America. There is nothing worse for a British reader than reading a book set in the UK, written by an American who just gets the details wrong. You can't just 'sprinkle' a few 'cor blimey guv'nor's into your dialogue and add a reference to the London Underground to create a convincing setting.

It is all the small details, added by someone who knows a place, that makes it real, and the small errors that a foreigner wouldn't spot, that could ruin the story (perhaps the character does math instead of maths, or plays soccer, or uses £100 notes to do their shopping, is a Manchester United fan even though they're from Sheffield, uses cockney rhyming slang when they're from Wales, drives from Carlisle to Cornwall in half an hour or speeds through London without hitting traffic – all things I've seen done and which have made me cringe).

When a character adds milk to their PG tips, walks through puddles without their wellies because of a sudden rain, takes a double-decker bus to school, has to do PE in kit from lost property, is sent to see the Headmaster, bunks off to buy lunch from the chippy, hits pot-holes in the car on the way to football practice, knows every word to *Wonderwall* by Oasis, eats toad-in-the-hole, sits on a plastic chair in a grimy A&E, buys a pencil-case from WH Smith, watches CBBC ... these are the tiny details which put them in a real time and place. These are also the kinds of things that probably wouldn't appear in a book written by someone who doesn't know life in the UK.

85

While I don't want to limit your imagination, it is generally best to set a contemporary story in a place you know. If not, if you must do a story set in Jamaica, although you've never been there, then do as much research as you can. Watch travel programmes set in Jamaica, use the internet for facts about living there (Wikipedia exists for a reason), read books by local authors set in their local area. If you have a Jamaican friend, speak to them about their experiences.

The same goes for a story set in the past. Research, research, research.

If you are making up a world, however, then hooray for you! The process can be such fun!

Sometimes a world can be as much of a central character in a novel, and as memorable as individual characters themselves. Who can think of *The Hunger Games* without the Capitol, *Harry Potter* without Hogwarts, *Mortal Engines* with predator cities or the *Lord of the Rings* without Middle Earth?

If you are creating a world from scratch, there are some brilliant resources to help you. I have written a questionnaire that you can use to make sure that you include all the key elements.

World Building Questionnaire

When is your story set? past, present or future?

Presents / past

In which universe is your story set? our earth, another planet, alternative version of earth etc

earth

In which country is your story set?

Great britain

What big issues does the country / world face? (In our world it might be environmental catastrophe caused by consumerism, or a global pandemic, in another world it could be something like an oncoming ice age, problems caused by the orbits of two moons etc.)

What are the politics of this country? How did it come to exist as a country, who governs it and how? Is it at peace, at war? Who are its allies / enemies?

How central is religion to life in this country? What is the religion of this country? What form does it take? What religious observances do its adherents have to make? How did it come about? What is the mythology of the religion? Is it monotheistic or a pantheon? Are there rival religions / sects? Is it at peace? Are there religious wars? How religious are your characters going to be?

What language do the people speak? Are there accents, different dialects, slang, swearing?

Describe the flora and fauna (plants and animals) of this world:

What level of technology has the world reached? Is it pre-industrial, industrial, computing, more advanced / sci fi? Environmentally friendly or not? What items would the characters find / need / use?

What form of transport is used on this world? How will the characters get around?

What is the food like?

Describe the architecture of the country in which your story is set. Is it familiar, alien, what is it based on, what building materials do they use?

How is society structured (is there a social hierarchy / caste system, is it capitalist, communist, socialist, a monarchy, a hegemony etc.)? Who is at the top of society and who is at the bottom?

How are families structured (standard nuclear, children taken from parents to be raised by the state, limited number of children permitted per family, children created in a lab etc)

How are children educated (if they are educated at all, are their schools, do they learn at home, do they board elsewhere, do they have to work and learn at the same time?)?

What kind of jobs do people have (if they have jobs?)

What is used for money (if they use money)?

What is used for entertainment? Are there books (which are most famous?), music (what sort and what instruments are played?), sports (what games?), card or board games (what are the rules of the most popular?)

Do your characters have hobbies / how do they spend their free time?

What are the laws? Are they religious or secular? How entwined is religion with the law? Who polices the populace and how? What punishments are there for transgressors?

How does the population deal with its sick? Are there hospitals? What level is medical science?

```



```

Anything else special about this world?

```



```

This is a pretty comprehensive questionnaire, which should help you a lot, but if you are writing a fantasy world, and want to go into even more detail, there is an amazing list of things to think about here, written by Patricia C. Wrede for the SFWA.

https://www.sfwa.org/2009/08/04/fantasy-worldbuilding-questions/

Once you have your world planned, there are few things to remember.

You must **be consistent**. If your character lives in a world of darkness, you can't have a scene where a character watches the sunrise. If your characters live in a world without rain, you can't have succulents growing in the garden, or puddles on the ground.

You must **stick with the rules** you create. If there is limited oxygen, you can't have your character running around without a mask, if your character is a vampire, you can't have her decide to go for a mid-day stroll or a day at the beach.

Do also **watch anachronisms** (things belonging to a period, or in this case place, other than that in which it exists).

You can't have a fantasy world in which people are using mobile phones, for example, unless you explain very clearly who built all the phone masts, where the factories are that produce the phones, who came up with the technology, who is mining the metals and so on. Same with cars or pretty much any modern technology. Similarly, why would there be horses and carts on a space station, or laser guns on a low-tech farming planet?

Related to this, think about how you have your characters speak, the similes and metaphors they use. Make sure that you don't accidentally use things from our world, that don't exist in this other plane you have created (more on simile and metaphor later).

When you have carefully planned your wonderful world, so that it is almost as real to you as your own front garden, you might feel compelled to tell the reader every tiny detail, but don't! You should treat your new made-up world just like you would a contemporary fiction piece.

The key is to make even the most unusual, alien, worlds feel real, by ensuring that they feel 'everyday' to *your character*. If your character lives in a future world, then flying to school in a shuttle should feel as humdrum to them as driving to school in a bus would to you. And just as you wouldn't spend ages describing a bus journey as part of your story (unless something essential to the plot happens on the bus), then you shouldn't spend ages describing the shuttle trip either.

What if your character is an adult in a fantasy world who commutes to work by Graklah? They would consider this as normal as your dad finds it to commute by car, so your character would not describe in great detail what a Graklah is and how he travels on it.

Good world building is subtle. It's the small details, as mentioned before. You could let the reader know what a Graklah is, subtly. *'Hey Snodgrout, your Graklah is chewing up the parking field, haven't you fed it this morning?'*

The Planning Bit

Now you have a character or characters, and the world they inhabit, and probably a few ideas regarding the storyline, which have grown out of all this planning, you will need to think about the structure of your story.

I *know*, you hate planning, you just want to *write*!

Some writers don't plan, it's true. This seems particularly the case with horror writers – Stephen King, Dean R Koontz, Steve Feasey – all examples of writers who are known for not plotting. I wonder if they operate on the basis that if they are shocked by something they are writing, then their audience will be too?

However, in my view, *not* planning is something that only a very experienced writer can do well.

Think of learning to write well, like learning to cook.

You have to use recipes when you are learning to cook, so that you know what works (and what doesn't). Only then can you make up your own (which reminds me of the time my son brought me a drink that he'd 'made up for me' consisting of freshly squeezed raw grapes, milk and tabasco! – I had to drink it with a smile).

Experienced writers who don't plot will have internalised so many plotting rules (perhaps by reading fiction widely, by reading non-fiction books like this one, or perhaps by being an ex-plotter) that they subconsciously follow them. They know instinctively what beats the story needs and where. If something isn't working, they will be able to fix it because they will be able to work out what is missing.

However, many experienced writers remain plotters. Charles Dickens was a careful plotter and I have read that JK Rowling had the whole of Harry Potter – all seven books - planned out and locked in a safe very early on. I personally am a strict plotter.

Plotter versus Pantster?

Funny as it may seem, these are actual industry terms. A plotter, obviously, is a writer who plans out their story before they write it. A pantster is a writer who flies by the seat of their pants (makes things up as they go along).

Do these scenarios feel familiar to you?

Your teacher asks you to write a 500-word story, you get to word 492, realise you are nowhere near tying up your story and write 'she woke up, it was all a dream'.

You are writing a story, and then halfway through, you think of a great idea, which could really change things. You don't want to start again, or forget the idea, so you chuck it in right there and then?

You have no idea who your story is going to end until you get there.

These are things that young pantsters commonly experience.

With a published novel, it is impossible for a reader to tell if the writer was a plotter or a pantster.

However, often a writer I am mentoring will send me a novel that feels as if it has had every idea thrown at it, including the kitchen sink. Ideas appear mid-way through with no preamble, a protagonist does something completely out of character, or the story takes a sudden left turn and I know immediately that writer is a pantster - making it up as they go along.

I always ask these writers to plan carefully before rewriting and planning always, without fail, improves their story.

I personally, am a plotter. If I wake up one morning with a character or a story idea, I let it simmer for a while. If the idea is still hanging around and bothering me a month or so later, I think it is likely a good one, so I will write a one-page summary of the story, called a synopsis, making sure to include all the important narrative high points (I'll explain this later in the chapter titled *One Page Summary*). At this point I usually send it to my agent.

If she likes the idea, I write my character pen pictures, do any supplementary character work, such as writing their full backstory and working on their voices, do the necessary research and world-building and complete a chapter outline. This means that I will write a paragraph or two for each chapter, detailing the important events of the chapter and adding in notes about any red herrings, real clues or foreshadowing that I want to include.

At this point I can tell if the story is going to work well and, if I think it is, I'll start writing my first draft. Because I've done all this planning, I can now write the novel quickly and fairly easily. My last two novels both took me eight weeks to write (to first draft), after the planning process was complete.

Of course, I am not completely proscriptive. If I think of a great idea while I'm writing, I will fit it in. If I need to do some research (as I often do mid-chapter) and I find out something fascinating that I want to include, I'll include it.

So, I plot, but do allow some flexibility. Writing is a creative process after all.

There are many good reasons to become a plotter.

1. Your stories will likely be better (honestly).
2. You can include things like foreshadowing, literary allusion, clues and red herrings because you know what is coming up next (and clever readers *love* these).
3. It is motivational – I know that if I've got to chapter ten, for example, then I'm halfway through (and I can have a little chocolatey celebration).
4. Plotting helps you plan your time. I always write a timetable when I have a deadline. Because I have written a chapter outline, I know exactly how much I need to write, how long the chapters are likely to be and therefore how much time I need to allocate for each. This means that I can timetable breaks in for myself (always important) and that I meet deadlines without the last-minute panic of being two days before the deadline and having a story that is showing no signs of wrapping up.
5. Plotting saves time. Many pantsters have to go back and reread what they've written so far to get back into the 'zone' each day. My writing time can be limited, so I need to be able to sit down and just get going.
6. Plotting helps with writer's block. If I already know where the story is going, I can write, even if I'm not in the mood. I don't have to be particularly creative, the writing doesn't have to be brilliant - I can go back and add sparkle to the text later once I have my mojo back.

So yes, I am going to suggest that you become a plotter at least until you get used to structuring a story.

Short stories

In this section we are going to talk about short stories and how to plan them. This is because short stories are awesome, in school it is what you are most likely to be writing and, if you want to enter competitions, short stories are a common requested format.

Unsurprisingly, short stories are different to novels in how you structure them, but some of the same rules will apply. First of all, if you're given a word count, I would think about structuring your story around that word count. Here is a suggestion for 500 words:

Word count	Include
100	Introduction (Hook and opening problem)
150	Rising action (confrontation)
150	Climax (peak of the action)
100	Resolution / twist

You will likely be familiar with these words and concepts because you will have done the story mountain at school.

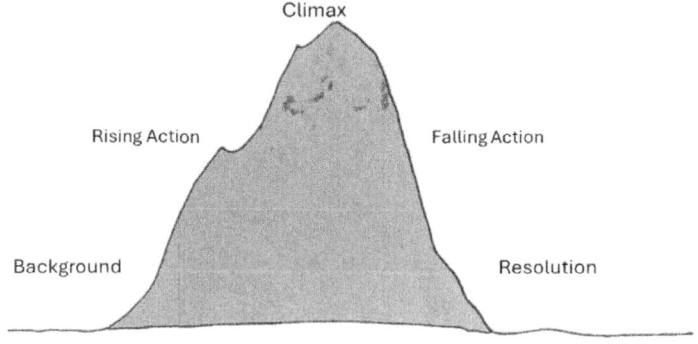

These are the things that I suggest you include in your plan for your short story:

Short story planning	
Characters (no more than three)	
Where and when is your story set?	
In what amount of time will your story take place?	
What message do you want the reader to leave with?	
Opening hook? (your first line that will make the reader ask questions)	
What is the main character trying to achieve?	
What happens if they fail?	
What stands in their way?	
How will they solve the problem?	
How do they achieve their goal?	
What is the twist / sudden surprise?	

More on all of these things coming up, don't worry!

Characters in a short story

You can design your characters just as we have already done, but the rule for a short story is that you *must not* include a cast of thousands. You literally don't have the space to spend any time introducing them properly or giving them space to operate. The best short stories have a limited number of characters. I would say that *two or three is ideal.* If you include more, you won't be able to do them justice.

The other thing about characters in a short story, is that it is sometimes a lot of fun to play with perspectives. Don't always pick the obvious character to write a short story about.

A lot of well-known stories are written from the point of view of unexpected characters. *Wicked* (Maguire), for example is set in Oz, but is written from the point of view of the wicked witch of the west, instead of Dorothy Gale.

If you're asked to write a short story about the coronation of Queen Elizabeth, for example, you could write about the event from her point of view, but it might be even more interesting to have, as your main character, the person charged with cleaning her crown (who accidentally drops and dents it, or loses it and has to find it in time), the person who has made her dress (and is working up to the last minute trying to hem it), or an orphan boy who desperately wants to see the coronation and who breaks into the cathedral and hides (does he get away with it?).

Timescale of a short story

Just as you shouldn't have a cast of thousands, with a short story it is an idea to restrict the timescale in which your story takes place to a *small snapshot of time*. It won't be easy to write an epic adventure spanning centuries with only 500 words, or even with 2,000-5,000 words (the commonest required lengths for adult short stories).

If you are asked to write a short story based on William the Conqueror, for example, you wouldn't write down everything that happened to him from birth to death. Instead, you would pick the few hours of his life that most interest you, and write a story based on those.

I would also always recommend starting your short story as near to the end of the events as possible. Think of events taking place over one day, or even a few hours.

Making your short story memorable

You want your short story to be memorable, something the reader will keep thinking about at odd times, even years later.

You can achieve this memorability by writing something beautiful, or with phrases that the reader will never forget.

You can achieve it by writing something shocking, or with a twist that surprises the reader.

You can achieve it by including a message or question that makes your reader think.

Many short stories contain a message, something the writer wants the reader to take away with them, an over-riding emotion, or something they want you to think about an issue. This is often given away in the twist at the end, but the whole story should be focused on achieving this aim.

Before writing you should **find your key emotion**. This is the feeling that you want your reader to be left with. A short story should have a single mood and every sentence must build towards it (more on creating mood in the chapter titled *Creating Atmosphere*).

Structure of a short story

Much like a novel, a short story can be told in three acts.

Act one: Introduction

In the Introduction you need to …

1. Hook the reader into your story -

    o   Begin with action that will draw us in.
2. Introduce the reader to your characters -

    o   Show us what they care about or are most afraid of.
3. Establish the setting and tone.
4. Make promises to the reader as to where the story is going.
5. Show us the problem that the character is going to have to solve.

    a.   What does your main character (protagonist) want to achieve?

    b.   Who or what is in their way?

    c.   What happens if they fail (stakes for failure)?

Look at the opening act of my story *The Tenth Man* (Published in *Now we are Ten* by Newcon Press):

> *'You've got the paperwork?' The nurse held out his hand. Or was he a nurse? My eyes went to the cuffs on his belt, the walkie-talkie.*

I stuttered a reply, offering the folder I had almost forgotten to bring in from the car. 'A letter from the university, permission from his wife, a note from his doctor.'

The story starts with a conversation. The opening line immediately sets the scene and undermines our comfort. What kind of nurse has cuffs and a walkie-talkie? Where are we? It also strongly suggests that at some point in the story things are going to go wrong.

Is turns out that the protagonist, Dean is at a mental hospital where he is hoping to interview a Professor, an expert in his field.

'I'm doing my PhD on his work, hoping to take it forward towards completion.'

We know where we are, who we are with, what the protagonist wants to achieve and what happens if he fails (he will be unable to complete his PhD).

The nurse then gives him a chilling warning about the Professor's illness and how it might affect Dean himself.

The message of the story is a warning about the danger of unthinking ambition. This is set up in the opening.

Act two: Confrontation

The protagonist should face a complication as they are moving along, often things get worse for them and they need to find ways to tip the scale in their favour.

- What is keeping your protagonist from achieving their goal?
- What are they going to do to solve their problem/s?

In *The Tenth Man*, the Professor has D.I.D. (multiple personalities) and every time Dean seems to be making progress, the Professor switches. Dean has to find a way to stabilise the Professor so that he can winkle out his knowledge. He does this by appealing to the mathematician inside of him, by correcting his work.

In *The Gift of the Magi* (O.Henry), the main character, Della, has only $1.87 to buy a Christmas gift for her husband. This grieves her, so in the second act of the story she looks for a solution. She realises that she can sell her beautiful hair, which reaches below her knees. She makes $20 from the sale and buys a gold chain for her husband's watch, the one valuable thing he owns.

Read this story here:

americanenglish.state.gov/files/ae/resource_files/1-the_gift_of_the_magi_0.pdf

At the end of the story, however, we discover that Jim, also desperate to buy his wife a Christmas present, has sold his gold watch to buy combs for his wife's beautiful hair. How ironic!

Act three: Resolution

Build to a satisfying conclusion that lives up to the promise you made early in the story.

- How does the main character achieve their goal?

- What is the twist – the sudden change / surprise that will remain with the reader?

- Always make sure there is a point to your story -
    - o   What can the reader take from your story?
    - o   In what way have the characters changed?

If you aren't sure how to end your story, ask yourself, **how would a *reader* want this story to end**?

Try using dialogue to end your story, or reveal a twist in the very last sentence, leaving the reader reeling.

A twist is the most effective way of making a story remain with a reader. This is because surprises are memorable and a good twist will make the reader think about the story and what happened in it, long after they have finished reading.

This is also the point at which you can reveal the true point behind writing your story.

In *The Tenth Man* it turns out that the professor has been manipulating Dean all along. At the end of the story Dean thinks that he has got what he wants from the Professor, but actually it is the Professor who has won and, as Dean leaves, the reader realises he is going to end the world with the knowledge he has acquired.

Read *The Lottery (1948) by Shirley Jackson:*

www.cusd200.org/cms/lib/IL01001538/Centricity/Domain/361/jacks
on_lottery.pdf

The moment you realise what the winner of the lottery gets, will remain with you forever. And this is the moment that you realise the writer was making a point about ridiculous traditions, and the damage that people can do, by doing things just because they've always been done that way.

Or read *The Landlady by Roald Dahl*

www.teachingenglish.org.uk/sites/teacheng/files/landlady_text.pdf

The ending is as creepy as they come, and it absolutely *hammers* home a message about the importance of observation!

Opening and closing a short story

Your first and last lines should be the strongest in your story. The first line needs to hook the reader in (make the reader ask questions, make them *need* to read on), the last line needs to leave them reeling.

And remember, this story is *short*, that means that every single word has to work as hard as possible. Don't write '*very tired*', when you can write '*exhausted*', don't write '*ran quickly*' when you can write '*sprinted*'.

Every sentence in your story must work hard too. Each has to reveal character or advance the action.

Read A Clean, Well-Lighted Place *by Ernest Hemingway* – not one word exists that doesn't serve the story:

https://learning.hccs.edu/faculty/samuel.huntington/engl130 2/materials-for-the-8-week-cinco-ranch-section/additional-readings-and-handouts/a-clean-well-lighted-place-by-ernest-hemingway/view

Rules for starting your story

- Start as close to the climax as you can.

- Never start on dreams (you don't want to confuse your reader or get them hooked on something that isn't part of your story).

- Never start with travel (it is usually boring).

- Never start with weather (see above).

- Never start with exposition (telling the reader what is going on – this too is boring).

- Find the first point of action in your story and start there -

  o An argument, a fight, a rant, a moment of drama, falling off a cliff, crashing a car, a robbery in progress … start with something exciting if you can.

Look at these two openings for the same story.

Opening 1
Micky rolled out of bed, slipped his feet into his slippers and wobbled his way into the bathroom, rubbing his eyes. He put the toothpaste on his toothbrush and cleaned his teeth while making faces at himself in the mirror. Then he washed his face and made his way downstairs. There he found a giant hole in the floor where his living room should have been.

Opening 2
Mickey stared. There was a hole. It was the exact size of his living room. He stared some more. The hole seemed to have no bottom and there was no sign of the things that should have been there. The sofa, the telly, grandad's chair. There was only a hole. "You guys." he shouted, with a wobble in his voice. "You guys?"

Which version of this story do you want to read?

- Always start with the moment Mickey finds the hole!

Writing Exercise
What kind of twist could you include at the ending of Mickey's story?
Why not write the rest of the story yourself?

Long stories

Now we have talked about how to plan a short story, we will look at novel-length stories.

Young people are as capable of committing to writing a full-length narrative as anyone else. One of the girls that this book is dedicated to, wrote several 40,000-word novels in her summer holidays - I mean, *wow*!

What I am going to assume going forward, is that the story you are writing is for young people (Mid-grade or Young Adult), as it really does take someone with life experience to write a novel for adults.

As you already know, I think it is essential to plan your story carefully, so what we are going to do in this section is look at how to plan a full-length novel. The first thing we looked at with short-story planning is word-counts, so we'll look at word-counts here too.

You might be surprised to hear that different types of story have different word counts and that it is actually important to stick within the word count range for your story type (genre). If you write too many words, or not enough words, you will find that agents and publishers are put off your story and may not even read it.

Or they might buy it, and then ask that you cut 20,000 words (this has happened to me). So, you might as well get it right from the start and plan the structure of your story with a word count in mind.

Word counts

Different age groups have different writing requirements in terms of content and word count.

Type of book	Usual word count	Example
Board book	0 -100	*Peepo*
Early picture book	0 - 500	*Goodnight Moon*
Picture books	50 – 1,000	*The Gruffalo*
Non-fiction picture books	500 – 2,000	*The Silly Book of Weird and Wacky Words*
Early readers	200 – 3,500 depending on age	*Horrid Henry's Stink bomb*
Chapter books	4,000 – 10,000	*Charlotte's Web*
Mid-grade	25,000 – 50,000	*Harry Potter and the Philosopher's Stone*
Young Adult	50,000 – 80,000	*Savage Island*
New Adult	70,000 – 90,000	*A Court of Thorns and Roses*

There are exceptions, especially for the fantasy or science-fiction genre (which, with the greater world building required are permitted greater lengths) but I wouldn't count on being an exception. I recommend staying within (or close to) the recommended word count for your age category. There are a lot of agents that will reject on atypical word count alone.

Now you know your word count, you can structure your story accordingly.

The structure of a novel is similar to the structure of the short story, in that there are usually three acts, and you should still think about things like the importance of the opening hook, but when writing a full-length novel, there are more narrative high points to know about.

If you're at school, or have been reading this book one chapter at a time, you'll know about the story mountain. What I'm going to show you now is how to *zoom in* on the story mountain, adding a few extra bits that will make your story even better!

In this section I am going to talk about something called a **narrative arc**. This is the term that people in the creative industry use to describe the trajectory of the journey the characters go on in a story. In the simplest terms it can be explained as involving a clear beginning, middle and end.

The beginning will establish a character in a particular situation (and face them with a problem or give them a goal).

The middle will involve the exploration and development of the situation (the problem getting worse or obstacles getting in the way of goal-achievement) until the character arrives at a crisis.

The end shows how the character emerges from the situation (solves the problem or puts it into perspective) and returns to normality, or a state better than before.

Now let me zoom in on that story mountain and add the missing detail.

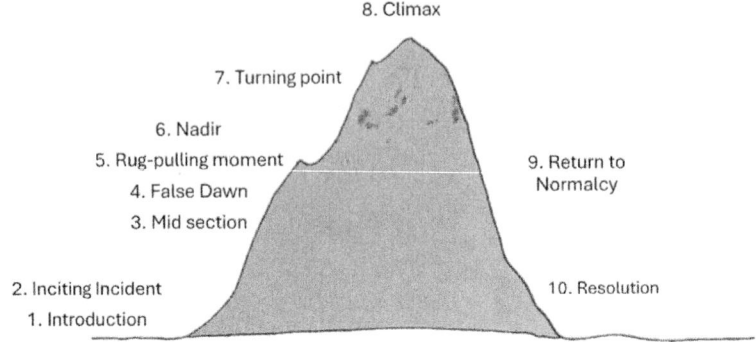

In the foothills, where you had 'Background', you now have 'Introduction' and 'Inciting Incident'. This is your **Act One**. I usually allocate three chapters for this part of the novel.

Introduction

In the introduction to your novel, you need to *introduce* your character and their world. Set the tone of the story and show us what kind of novel this is going to be.

Often it is best to show your character in their ordinary life, *before* their adventure begins. This gives your characters something to lose (or escape from) and something to return to, if need be.

Think about Harry Potter - does he start his story at Hogwarts? No, he starts it living his ordinary life, in the cupboard under the stairs, with the Dursleys.

We start a few beats *before* the main adventure, to show the reader *who* this character is, to get us to love them and invest in them, and also so that we can see how the adventure that is going to follow is going to change them.

At the end of the story, we will often see the character go back to their ordinary life (or a new version of it), but they will be a different person. If you can show who they are at the start, your reader can make that comparison. It's all about *character arc* really.

A story in which your character does not learn anything, or change, is a story that is unlikely to work. As a reader we want to know that we have invested our time for a reason, and that the character has therefore learned a lesson.

Perhaps someone who is selfish at the beginning, becomes self-sacrificing by the end, perhaps someone who plays pranks has learned how to see things from other perspectives, perhaps someone who is judgmental has learned to walk a mile in someone else's shoes and so on …

In order to be clear that there has been a change, therefore, we need to see who they are at the start. We need to see the selfish character being selfish (perhaps their mum asks them to babysit their young sibling, but they refuse because they'd rather do something else, or they grudgingly agree but keep playing on their x-box). We need to see the judgemental character judging others (perhaps they see someone at school who is unwashed and smelly and makes a comment).

Emma in Jane Austen can be very judgemental and makes a lot of mistakes because of it, but we still love her, and she learns her lesson by the end.

https://youtu.be/qIjob8Zxf-g

Although this may seem like you are setting up a character to be disliked, remember your character's minor flaw will be matched with two strengths.

So, if your character is kind and loyal, but can be judgemental, you could show them sneering at the dirty school friend, but then insisting that they come to their house for dinner and a shower, where they learn that the friend's parents have died, and they are trying to pretend everything is fine to avoid being sent to live with a cruel aunt and uncle.

If your character is funny and brave, but also selfish, you can show how awful they feel that their little brother gets hurt on their watch, and all the things they do to make up for it.

In the film *Labyrinth*, the girl hates being asked to babysit for her little brother, so she asks the goblin king to take him away, when he actually does, the girl does everything she can to get her brother back.

Don't forget to include pat the dog, or undeserved suffering when introducing your character.

Just because you are starting your story with your character's ordinary life, it doesn't mean you have to start it in a boring place.

Ordinary doesn't mean boring. An astronaut's ordinary life might be living on the ISS – does that sound boring to you? A racing driver's ordinary life will include speeding around the track – does that sound boring? Your character's ordinary life can still include exciting action, arguments, strange encounters and so on.

My novel *Windrunner's Daughter,* which started life as a Mid-grade adventure (with dragons) and ended up as a Young Adult adventure (set on Mars), got me an agent. My agent said it was the strongest opening they'd ever read. So, what did I do to make the opening so strong?

In it, I started with my main character dangling from the edge of a cliff and yes, this *was* an incident from her ordinary life. Wren lives at the top of the cliff and is running to town to get medicine for her sick mother, when she slips from the path and falls. The real adventure doesn't start until chapter three, when she realises that she'll have to get help for her mother elsewhere, but I started with a heart-in-the-mouth, mini-adventure, which showed that Wren is brave and self-reliant, but way too reckless for her own good.

In this opening I showed the reader that the story will be an action-filled adventure, I made it clear where it was set (Wren has a pretty good view from the top of that cliff) and I showed the reader her goal (save her sick mother). I also made it clear what happens if she fails to achieve this goal (her mother will die).

Once you have introduced your character you must make it clear what they want for themselves (Wren wants to save her mother and, on the way, she'll learn to be less reckless and more reliant on others).

To summarise, a good **introduction** will –
1. Start with the character in their ordinary life, but NOT doing something boring, instead having a *mini-adventure*.
2. Use this mini-adventure to highlight the character's strengths and flaw.
3. Use pat the dog and / or undeserved suffering.
4. Show the reader what the character wants out of life (or most wants to avoid).
5. Show the reader where we are.

Once you have done this, you then move onto the next part of the mountain, the **Inciting Incident.**

Inciting Incident

The inciting incident is the moment that your protagonist is propelled into the main action. In *Star Wars A New Hope*, Luke's mini-adventure (where we find out who he is) is his discovery of R2D2 and the message from Leia, which tells him she needs helps from Obi Wan Kenobi. Luke takes R2D2 to 'Old Ben' and leaves.

https://youtu.be/5cc_h5Ghuj4

However, when he gets back home, to his farm, he finds that it has been destroyed and that his aunt and uncle have been murdered by stormtroopers.

https://youtu.be/yV2osP3vQQA

This is the incident that sends him into the arms of the Rebel Alliance and starts his adventure with Leia and Han Solo. This is the inciting incident.

In *Harry Potter* it is the receipt of his letter of acceptance into Hogwarts.

In *The Hunger Games*, it is Katniss offering to take her sister's place in the games.

In *Raising Hell* it is when Ivy agrees to save Norah's life.

When the inciting incident is taking place, you *must* also show the reader your character's goal and the stakes for failure.

You would be AMAZED how many aspiring writers miss out these absolute KEY parts of the novel.

The character's GOAL is what is going to drive them through the adventure, from the inciting incident to the end of the story. Without it the story is nothing more than ... stuff that happens to someone.

The STAKES FOR FAILURE are what will happen if your character fails. We need to know this because the goal has to feel important. We must root for the main character to achieve their goal, which means that we need to know the terrible thing that will happen if they fail to achieve it.

Harry's goal is to defeat Voldemort, the wizard who murdered his parents. If he fails, the evil wizard will take over the world and kill or enslave muggles and half-bloods (like Hermione and her parents)

Katniss's goal is to survive the Hunger Games and get back to her family. This morphs into making sure that both she *and Peter* survive, which will mean tricking the system. If she fails, they will die.

In *Savage Island* Ben's goal is to make sure that the team all survive to get away from the island. If he fails, of course he or his friends may die, but for Ben, more importantly, he will have failed to protect his brother.

In *Raising Hell* Ivy's goal is to get rid of the hellhound and save Norah. If she fails Norah and, it turns out, a lot of other people, will die.

To summarise, a good **inciting incident** will –

1. Drag your character into the main adventure.
2. Show the reader what the main problem is that needs solving.
3. Make it clear what the character's primary goal is.
4. Make it clear what will happen if they fail to achieve that goal.

The next part of the novel, in which we are climbing your story mountain, is the mid-section. Now we are into **Act two.**

Mid-Section

This, rather boringly titled section, is where you will explore the situation, showing the development of the problem and what the character/s will try to do to overcome it.

In *Savage Island*, for example, once the characters realise the seriousness of their situation, they decide to -

1. Make weapons for protection.
2. Try to find the adult organisers of the event who will be able to help them.
3. Move through the check points without completing them.
4. Look for ways off the island.

This section is all about letting the protagonist explore their options, showing them becoming stronger and realising what they really need, and showing us who or what the antagonist (bad guy) is (or their representative/s).

Think about *The Lord of the Rings*. In the introduction we see Frodo in his ordinary life in the Shire. Then he receives the ring and finds out that it is the 'One Ring to Rule Them All', that the evil Sauron is searching for. He is told that he must destroy the ring by throwing it into a particular volcano (inciting incident). So, Frodo and his friends set off on a journey to Mordor, to destroy the ring. In the mid-section, they are attacked by Sauron's Ringwraiths and meet protectors who will help them on their journey.

To summarise, your **mid-section** must

1. Explore the situation – make it clearer what the problem is and what is standing in your protagonist's way.

2. Show how the protagonist is going to try and solve this problem / achieve their goal.

The next section is the false dawn. In this section it appears that everything is going well.

False Dawn

Here the character gains confidence. What they are doing is *working*. Everything is going to be *all right*!

In *Savage Island*, Ben and his friends are pounding through the checkpoints, getting ahead of the other teams and looking forward to finding adult help.

In *Star Wars A New Hope,* Luke has rescued Leia.

In *The Hunger Games*, alliances have been formed, and it looks like Katniss can win.

We need to give the character this upward beat because we're about to pull the rug out from under them. Writing a successful story is about those moments in which pace and tone changes - moments of pause, of celebration. Right now, the character is likely riding high. All is well, the goal is going to be achieved, we can take a moment to breathe.

In a romance film, this is the moment the boy gets the girl (or the girls gets the boy, or girl gets the girl, or boy gets the boy and so on), but it's only halfway through and we *know* something is about to go wrong!

To summarise, a good **false dawn** will -

1. Make it seem as if what the protagonist is doing is *working*.

2. Give the protagonist false confidence.

3. Give the reader a break in pace and tone before the big dip of the rug-pulling moment.

Next of course, we have the rug-pulling moment.

Rug-Pulling Moment

In a Romantic Comedy there will be a misunderstanding or piece of miscommunication, or the girl discovers something the boy has lied about, and Boy Loses Girl.

In *Savage Island,* despite fighting their way through the checkpoints, Ben and co, discover that there is no adult help to be had. In fact the adults are behind it all.

In *Star Wars A New Hope*, Darth Vader and battles and kills Obi Wan Kenobi.

This rug-pulling moment should be something unexpected (but not totally out of the blue) and should tip the character into peril or despair.

Did the reader in *Savage Island* really think there would be an adult at the end who would solve all the problems? The characters were always deluding themselves. There were clues throughout that, not only was no-one going to solve this for them, but that the adults in the picture were going to be the ones in control of the whole mess.

This down beat is needed because the next section is the nadir. The Character's darkest hour. And we need this before the climax, to make the climax really seem like a big deal! Big highs can only come after big lows, as you know if you've ever ridden on a roller-coaster!

To summarise, a good **rug-pulling moment** will -

1. Tear the rug out from the protagonist – show them that what they were doing *has not worked.* They were on the wrong path the whole time!

2. Not be out of the blue or completely unexpected.

3. Lead into the most emotionally impactful scenes of the story.

The rug-pulling moment is followed by the Nadir – this is the character's darkest hour.

Nadir

In your Romantic Comedy this is the moment the main character walks through the rain all alone or sits by a window staring out at the rain (there is usually rain) while a sad song is playing. If you've ever seen *Friends*, this is Rachel sitting by her window, staring into the rain while U2's *With or Without You* plays.

https://youtu.be/XAznrm7BAcg

In *Savage Island*, this is the moment Ben discovers who the real bad guy is and that he wants Ben's brother, Will. Ben discovers some terrible things about himself and one of his friends dies.

In *Star Wars A New Hope*, Obi Wan Kenobi is killed by Vader and it looks as if the Rebel base is going to be wiped out by the Death Star.

https://youtu.be/8kpHK4YIwY4

This is the moment that the reader should be crying for your character (or at least sniffing a little, certainly feeling sorry for them!).

To summarise, a good **nadir** will -
1. Be a black moment. The character is dealing with the failure of their plans, and not coping well.
2. Be the lowest point of the story, emotionally speaking.

Because after the nadir, something changes, the character works out how they really can solve their problem. This is **Act three**.

The Turning Point

Here the character discovers the way to dig themselves out of danger, often by turning the original problem on its head, changing their attitude, or accepting a possibility they have previously rejected. I particularly like it when the turning point refers back to the character's strengths or weakness or something they have learned or gained in the course of the adventure so far.

In *Savage Island*, Ben accepts that it is his brother's turn to protect *him.*

In *Star Wars A New Hope*, Luke realises that he can fly his x-wing to the heart of the death star and use the force to exploit its weakness.

In *Harry Potter*, Harry realises that he must allow himself to be killed by Voldemort but that the Deathly Hallows can help bring him back.

> To summarise, a good **turning point** will -
> 1. Include the real solution to the problem / route to achieving the character's goal.
> 2. Not be out of the blue or completely unexpected (it should have been seeded earlier on).

Once the character has worked out how to solve the problem we move into the climax.

Climax

In *Star Wars, A New Hope* this is the moment that Luke destroys the death star.

https://youtu.be/KuKqcfO31is

In *The Hunger Games*, it is the moment that Katniss threatens to commit suicide alongside Peter, thereby forcing the Capitol to save both of them if they want a winner for their parade.

This is the moment that that your protagonist beats the antagonist and achieves their goal (or if you are writing a tragedy or horror, they might fail in their mission), emerging triumphant.

Even if you are writing a tragedy or horror that ends badly for the protagonist, however, the climax should contain an element of the protagonist winning – they've learned a lesson, they've changed, their death frees them, their sacrifice saves someone else.

To summarise, a good **climax** will -
1. Be the most exciting point in the book - the highest point of tension.
2. Involve the main character emerging (at least in some way) triumphant.

Finally, a resolution.

Return to Normalcy / Resolution

Many aspiring writers miss out the resolution, which is as important as the introduction. This shows what life is like after the climax. It should tie-up loose ends and, in many cases, send the adventurer back into their ordinary life, a changed person.

In each *Harry Potter* (except the last), Harry ends up back at the Dursley's, (where he started), where he is more able to stand up for himself each time. In the last, we see what life was like after the defeat of Voldemort.

The resolution doesn't even have to be that long, in *Star Wars A New Hope*, it is the moment that everyone gets medals.

https://youtu.be/sraqNvbC7oo

But it does need to be long enough to answer all the questions the reader has and give them a chance to see the character settled and say goodbye to them. It is terrible when a book cuts off too early. It feels as if your best friend is being torn away from you.

This resolution should also highlight how the character has changed during the course of their adventure. Perhaps your hero encounters a bully, who terrified them in the opening, but who they can now completely dismiss as beneath their notice. Perhaps the judgemental character seeks forgiveness, or the selfish character offers to babysit for their baby brother twice a week so their exhausted mother can have a break, or take a class.

To summarise, a good **resolution** will -

1. Tie up loose ends.

2. Answer all the reader's questions.

3. Give the reader a chance to say goodbye.

4. Show the reader how the character has changed since the introduction.

One page Summary

So back to what I said I did when I told you I was a planner – that I write a one-page summary (or synopsis) of my story. This page contains the following information, one paragraph per section:

One page summary
Title
Introduction
Inciting Incident
Mid section
False Dawn
Rug-pulling moment
Nadir
Turning point
Climax
Resolution
Key themes / message of the story

Narrative point of view

The next thing to plan before you can start writing, is which perspective you would like to write from.

That means will you be writing like this?

I went to the shops, I bought a bag of apples.

Or like this?

She went to the shops, she bought a bag of apples.

In other words, will your reader be experiencing your story through the inner thoughts of a character (first person), or from the perspective of an observer (third person)?

Point of view is the angle that the story is viewed through. For example, if you wanted to rewrite the story of Cinderella, you could do it from different angles.

In the voice of Cinderella herself – what is she thinking?

In the voice of the wicked stepmother – was she really just misunderstood? What does she really want for her daughters?

In the voice of a step-sister - how does she feel about being 'the ugly one'? What does she really want? Does she go along with her mother or try to stop her behaviour?

In the voice of the prince – how does it feel to find the girl of your dreams and then lose her?

In the voice of an impartial observer – What does the person who has to carry the shoe through the town think of what is going on?

The point of view that you use to tell a story can influence how the reader feels about the events of the story.

The important thing to know when choosing a perspective is that you shouldn't change your mind partway through. You shouldn't switch from first person to third and you shouldn't jump from one head to another (unless you need to write a chapter from a different point of view – more on that shortly).

> Pick the character who is going to be telling the reader the story, choose the way they will tell the story, then stick with it.

As this is a book for those of you who want more information than you'd get in school, I am going to tell you about all the possible perspectives you could choose to write from, but do be aware that the most common perspectives, especially when writing YA or MG, are first person present and third person past, so I would recommend choosing between these two.

First person past

I walked into the room. The empty safe made me want to be sick, but instead I pulled out my notepad.

First person present

I walk into the room. The empty safe makes me want to be sick, but instead I pull out my notepad.

Both of these forms of first person are fine, but you must remain consistent throughout when writing your story, don't switch between past and present. It's an easy mistake to make, even for experienced writers. In fact, the last book I wrote, I realised after I sent it into my publisher, that I'd started with first person past and then accidentally and for no apparent reason, switched to first person present halfway through. I had to do a very quick and super-annoying, rewrite of the first half!

Pros and cons of writing in first person

Pros	Cons
Can convey inner thoughts, so your reader knows what your character is thinking. Most often used in YA fiction, where main characters can be quite introspective – musing on what has happened to them and what it means. Enables very swift and effective immersion into the main character. Simple mechanics – you know from whose point of view every scene will be told.	Limits the information the reader can know because new experiences are only relayed through only one person / perspective (for example, if the thief is coming up behind the detective, there is no way for the reader to know this until the detective does). It's harder to develop side characters and sub-plots about them. The reader must like the voice, or they'll dislike the story. Some people criticise first person, as not being a particularly 'literary' way of writing.

Second person

You walk into the room. The sight of the empty safe makes you feel sick, but you pull out your notepad.

Probably the most famous example of a second person narrative is *Bright Lights Big City* by Jay MacInerny.

Pros and cons of writing in second person

Pros	Cons
Puts the reader in the place of the main character.	You can only share with the reader what the narrator knows (same as with first person).
Most often used in choose your own adventure fiction or self-help books (rarely seen elsewhere).	It's harder to develop side characters and sub-plots.
Can also be used when the narrator is writing to 'you' e.g. *Dear Diary, you are my only friend ....*	The reader must like the voice, or they'll dislike the story. Unusual, and so might be distracting to the reader.
Can have a striking effect because it is rarely seen in standard fiction.	

Third person present, omniscient point of view

Third person is when you use the pronouns he / she / they.

Detective Smith walks into the room, sees the empty safe and pulls out his notepad. He looks so calm, thinks Bill.

Third person present is the viewpoint most common in screenplays.

Pros and cons of writing in third person present

Pros	Cons
Most often used in screenplays	Does not, as a rule, work well in novels, as people's natural tendency is to think in third person past tense.
Can have a striking effect because it is rarely seen in standard fiction.	
Can show the reader things that the main character does not see.	Causes sense of disconnect – harder for reader to engage.

Third person present, restricted point of view

Detective Smith walks into the room, sees the empty safe and pulls out his notepad.

Very much the same as above, generally only used in screenplays.

Pros and cons of writing in third person present, restricted

Pros	Cons
Most often used in screenplays Can have a striking effect because it is rarely seen in standard fiction. Simpler mechanics as you know who's point of view you are writing a scene from at all times.	Does not, as a rule, work well in novels, as people's natural tendency is to think in third person past tense. Causes sense of disconnect – harder for reader to engage. Cannot show the reader things that the main character does not see.

Third person past

Detective Smith walked into the room, saw the empty safe and pulled out his notepad.

From the time we first learn to tell others about the events of our lives, we do this in the past tense, because that's the way in which events play out. We go to school, we meet our friends, we go home, we tell our parents about our day in the past tense because it happened in the past.

Third-person, past-tense stories therefore have the advantage of feeling very natural.

This natural, logical method of relating events enables the reader to believe that the past-tense fiction they're reading is believable, precisely because the point-of-view technique being used mimics the way in which they hear stories from all sources.

This is probably the most widespread form of narration you will find in the books you read. It is particularly common in Mid-grade novels.

Third Person past, omniscient

Detective Smith walked in the room, saw the empty safe and pulled out his notepad. Behind him, the thief climbed out of the window.

In this point of view the narrator knows everything about everyone in the story – like a God.

Pros and cons of writing in third person past

Pros	Cons
Common form in fiction, so familiar to the reader.	Not as quick to immerse the reader in the character – can be difficult to establish connection.
Imitates how readers tell their own stories e.g. *What did you do at school today?* *We had maths and Bohan snorted milk out of his nose at break time. Mrs Smith tried not to laugh, but we all heard her.*	Can be confusing to the reader – who's point of view is a scene being shown from.
Helps suspension of disbelief / is believable.	
Can show the reader things that the main character does not see.	
Allows you to jump from character to character, revealing alternating ways to look at the conflict.	

Third person past, limited

Detective Smith walked in the room, saw the empty safe and pulled out his notepad. He felt sick, but he kept his expression calm.

Here, as with first person, the point of view is limited to only one character. The narrator experiences only what this character experiences and the character is most commonly the protagonist.

Pros	Cons
Common form in fiction, so familiar to the reader.	Limits the information the reader can know because experiences are only relayed through one person's perspective.
Imitates how readers tell their own stories.	
Is believable.	
Helps the reader get to know the main character well.	
You always know who's point of view to use in a scene.	
The reader always knows who's point of view is being shown.	

I recommend either first person, or third person restricted for effective writing for young people.

Head-hopping versus using more than one narrator

Once you have chosen your perspective, you mustn't change your mind part way through and, especially, you should avoid 'head hopping'.

In third-person past limited and first-person present (the two most common forms of narration in the novels you will have read) the narrator sticks to using one character's point of view within any given scene.

If your story is written in third-person past limited and you get inside multiple character's thoughts, or see through multiple character's perspectives in the same scene, then you're head-hopping.

Here is an extract from my own *Phoenix Burning* (told in third-person past from Toby's point of view):

Toby squinted as he followed Dee and Hiko on to the deck, the bright sunshine in stark contrast to the gloom of the mess hall. It took a moment for his eyes to adjust, then the changes that the pirates had made to the Phoenix came into focus.

'Toby, good to see you out in the fresh air.' Marcus swung down from the rigging.

'You've done so much in two days!' Toby looked up. 'You've already finished the retractable weather shield we designed.'

A tall pole rose over his head. Around it a series of curved metal panels made from hammered out car-bonnets hung like a skirt.

'How does it work?' Hiko touched one of the panels.

This scene is shown from Toby's point of view – every action, word and observation is his alone.

Now I am going to rewrite this (badly) to include head-hopping.

Toby squinted as he followed Dee and Hiko on to the deck, the bright sunshine in stark contrast to the gloom of the mess hall. It took a moment for his eyes to adjust, then the changes that the pirates had made to the Phoenix came into focus.

Marcus was delighted to see Toby squinting in the sunlight. He swung down from the rigging, his hands sore from the rough rope. 'Toby, good to see you out in the fresh air.'

Toby looked up, he could barely believe how much Marcus had achieved. 'You've done so much in two days!' He pointed. 'You've already finished the retractable weather shield we designed.'

Dee nodded, surprised, as she looked at the tall pole that rose over head. Around it a series of curved metal panels made from hammered out car-bonnets hung like a skirt.

Hiko was amazed. How was it possible that they had finished all of this? 'How does it work?' He touched one of the panels.

Who here is telling the story? Who is seeing the action and describing events? There's a bit from Toby's viewpoint, a bit from Marcus, a bit from Dee, a bit from Hiko. In one moment you're behind Toby's eyes, then you're in Marcus's head, feeling his sore hands, then back to Toby, dizzyingly swung over to Dee and then to the Hiko to feel his amazement.

When you change from one character's thoughts and observations to another's you're changing the storyteller. Unless this is handled carefully, it can disorient the reader.

Even in third person omniscient (where the narrator is God-like, seeing and knowing all) head-hopping is to be avoided. The narrator in third person omniscient sees all, knows all and reports on the thoughts of characters *from a distanced position.* As soon as the narrator steps closer and tells the story from the character's perspectives, it is no longer third-person omniscient and it is head-hopping.

Editors don't like head-hopping. It sets fuzzy rules, so the reader doesn't know what to expect or how to get comfortable. It pulls readers out of the flow of the narrative and can make them need to re-read passages. Head-hopping creates disengaged readers.

This doesn't mean you can't use more than one voice to tell a story. My novel *Cruel Castle* (the sequel to *Savage Island*) is told from *four* different perspectives – Grady's, Ben's, Lizzie's and Will's. However, each character gets their own chapter. I do not head-hop.

This works because -

1. I establish the rules early. Each character has their own set of chapters and each chapter heading tells the reader who we are with. It is clear that I am using these four different narrative viewpoints to tell different parts of the story.
2. I don't overlap – I keep the action linear. I choose the person most appropriate to reveal each incident in the story to avoid repeating events.
3. The characters are often separated, and I need the reader to know what is going on in the different locations.
4. Each character has their own distinct voice (it is very clear to the reader who is speaking to them).
5. A big part of the story is unpicking the trauma inflicted on each character by the events of *Savage Island*.

The Writing Bit

Openings and Hooks

By now you should know your main character/s almost as well as you know yourself. You should have done your research into, or carefully created your world. You should have a clear storyline plotted out and which you can follow. You should have chosen your narrative viewpoint – which character is going to tell the story and how they will tell it.

Now you can start writing … or can you?

Beating writer's block

With all the prep work you've done, you should be able to dive gratefully into writing, like it's a cool pool on a hot day!

Yippee!!

However, even with all of this, some people find the process of getting started with the actual writing quite difficult.

Here are my tips for getting over 'writer's block'.

1. If you haven't already planned out your storyline, give that a go. Having a plan is the easiest way to get over writer's block. Once you know what needs to happen, you can get on and make it happen!

2. Don't start at the beginning. Sometimes the pressure of coming up with that perfect opening can be quite daunting, so don't start there. Find a scene that excites you (it could even be the climax) and write that. Once you've got going, you'll find it a lot easier to go back and write the opening.

3. Or start *before* the beginning. If your story starts with your character dangling from a cliff, start earlier. Show your character finding her mum sick, realising she needs to get medicine, running down the path, slipping and catching herself, then dangling from the cliff. Then – and this is crucial – just delete everything that happened before the moment that things got exciting. This is like taking a run-up!

4. Take the pressure off yourself. Remind yourself that you are doing this because you love writing. You don't have to be the next William Shakespeare, or JK Rowling.

5. Allow yourself to take a break – take a bath, go for a walk, go on holiday even! Let your brain switch off from all

that planning, all those to-do lists. Eventually the writing bug with catch back up with you and you can get going.

Now that you are over your writer's block, it really is time to start writing.

Hooks

Imagine a fish. It is swimming around in its lake. One Sunday a lot of fishermen turn up. They all bait their hooks and cast their lines. Which fisherman is going to catch the fish? The one who has put the tastiest piece of bait on the end of their hook, of course!

Now imagine a reader. She is wondering around a book shop, trying to decide what to buy with the book token she (very luckily) received for her birthday. She looks at the front covers of the books, she reads the blurb on the back covers. Then she opens each book that interests her and reads the opening line.

Which book does she buy? The one with the opening that makes her want to read on, of course.

Yes, opening lines are crucial. This is called the hook (remember our fish!).

Your first line has to hook your reader. How? It should **make them want more information**.

Look at the opening sentence of *Savage Island*.

'What would you do for a million pounds?'

Immediately you know that the story is going to be about people doing something for a million pounds. But what?

Here are the questions this might cause the reader to ask: Who is asking this question? Who is being asked? Why are they asking? Is this hypothetical, or real - do they have a million pounds to offer? Where has this money come from? What are they going to ask the other person to do? What are they willing to do for the money?

It also challenges the reader to think – what would *I* do for a million pounds? You know that when reading the novel, you will be constantly challenged to think, would I do this? Would I go this far?

Look at the opening line of *The Weight of Souls*

Dead men take me to the nicest places!

As a reader you immediately ask who is narrating this? Are there real dead men here? How can a dead person take someone somewhere? Is the narrator being literal (is she in a nice place), or sarcastic (is she in a horrible place)? How did she get there? Why is she there? Who are the dead men?

This sets up the story well, because it is a story about a girl who sees ghosts and the dreadful things that happen to her as a result.

Look at the opening lines of your favourite stories. Why do they work?

154

So, now we know that **good story openings make your reader want more information.**

Another way to open a story strongly is with a **bold statement**. The reader may or may not agree with the statement, but they know the rest of the novel will be exploring it – proving or disproving it.

> *Happy families are all alike; every unhappy family is unhappy in its own way.* (Anna Karenina)

> *It is a truth universally acknowledged, that a single man in possession of a good fortune must be in want of a wife.* (Pride and Prejudice)

If you can't use a bold general statement, then a simple **statement of fact** can also work well.

> *Toby was going blind.* (Phoenix Rising)

> *I am an invisible Man.* (Invisible Man)

These still raise questions (Why is Toby going blind? Can this be stopped? Is the invisible man talking literally or metaphorically? How / why is he invisible? What is his story?) and can have quite an impact on the reader, even if they are not as memorable as a bold statement.

The best first lines can also introduce a **strong narrator's voice** this is easiest if you are using first person narration.

> *Before my back hit the headboard, I slammed on the sidelight. The bulb illuminated every corner of the room. There were no riflemen in the doorway. (*Angel's Fury*)*

Look at the opening of *The Color Purple* or *The Catcher in the Rye*, for some excellent examples.

Finally, you could **announce that you are going to tell a story**:

> *This is the saddest story I have ever heard. (*The Good Soldier*)*
>
> *Once upon a time ... (*all good fairy stories!*)*

Look at the opening of Italo Calvino's *If on a Winter's Night a Traveller*, for another famous example.

To summarise, **strong opening lines** (hooks):
1. Make the reader want more information.
2. Can be a bold general statement, which we may or may not agree with.
3. Can be a statement of fact.
4. Can contain a strong voice.
5. Could announce that you are going to tell a story.

Opening Scene

After the first line, you must dive into the rest of your opening scene.

There are several different ways you can write a strong opening:

1. Present an out- of-the-ordinary situation.
2. Pose an essential question.
3. Plunge into an exciting action sequence.
4. Use interesting language or a strong appealing voice.

Ideally you should employ a mixture of these.

Key things to *avoid* are starting a novel with:

1. Travelling.
2. The weather.
3. A dream.
4. Lots of exposition.

One of the best pieces of writing advice I was given when I was starting out (thank you, Nik Perring) was this: read your novel from the beginning. When you get to the moment the action starts, the moment you think 'wow yes, this is exciting', then *this* is the start of your novel. Delete everything else before this point.

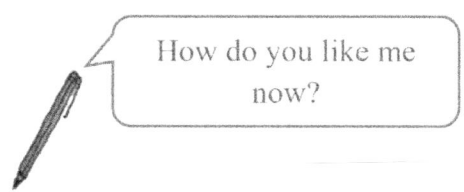

The Problem with Prologues

Some writers use prologues. A prologue is the bit of your novel that comes before the main story and is used to explain important information that doesn't follow the time-flow of the rest of your book.

It should be entirely separate to the main story that begins in Chapter One, *or* written from the perspective of a character whose point of view doesn't occur in the main story.

In crime novels, the prologue is often written from the perspective of a murder victim, while the rest of the novel is from the point of view of the detective character. In novels set in a world that is distant from our own, it can set up the rules of that world.

Unless you are writing a crime novel, however, I would recommend that you avoid writing a prologue.

You may think you need a prologue, but you can be quite creative coming up with ways to avoid it. When I was writing *Phoenix Rising* I created a world that was set in the future, after an environmental disaster and the eruption of the Yellowstone super-volcano. It was essential that the reader know how the world came about, otherwise a lot of story elements would be nonsensical, but any prologue would be either have to be a 100-page story about the end of the world (no good), or a super long (and probably very dull) historical treatise (no good). In place of a prologue, then, I decided to write as series of extracts from newspaper articles and memos.

If you can find a way to avoid writing a prologue, even a creative way, I would suggest that you should. The problems with prologues are numerous:

1. Often the information that appears in the prologue can easily be included elsewhere, for example your character could find an old letter, have a conversation or, if you are Harry Potter, experience a vision in the pensieve!

2. Your prologue could be *too good*. I have read books before where I have been so engaged with the prologue, that when that character or situation is abandoned in favour of the main story, I have been so upset that I have resented the main character and been unable to engage with Chapter one. If there is a risk your reader might want more of that great prologue character, or exciting prologue situation, then you're making a mistake to include it.

3. Some writers see prologues as a convenient way of world-building or telling the reader backstory. If your prologue is a dull history lesson, then cut it.

4. Some readers (and that includes editors and agents) hate prologues. In which case it is best not to risk presenting them with one!

5. Many readers hate prologues so much that they skip them and go straight to chapter one, which means that all the information in your prologue, which you thought was so important, is completely missing the reader.

Goal and Stakes for Failure

Now you are into chapter one. You've written a wonderful first line (opening hook) and an opening scene that engages the reader.

Something that I have already said bears repeating. *Your character needs a goal and stakes for failure.*

Make it very clear what your character wants / needs to achieve, and what happens if they fail.

Frodo (*TLOTR*) needs to destroy the ring, or the evil Sauron will take over Middle Earth.

Harry (*Harry Potter*) needs to defeat Voldemort, or he will take over the world.

Cassie (*Angel's Fury*) needs to find out why she keeps having her nightmares, or she will go insane.

Toby (*Phoenix Rising*) needs to save his father, or he'll be killed.

And so on.

The reader needs to know what the character's goal is and what happens if they fail, so that we can cheer them on. This goal should be what *drives the narrative*. Every decision your character makes in the course of the story will be in the service of achieving this goal.

Without a goal and stakes for failure, you are just giving us a bunch of stuff that happens to someone. That's not a story, it's a fictional biography.

Pacing

Books written for young people tend to be fast-paced and full of tension. This is partly because authors are competing with Netflix and x-box for their attention, partly because a fast-paced book full of tension is usually a great story that will attract a publisher.

In fast-paced books the action comes thick and fast, and each chapter ends on a cliff-hanger or presents an unanswered question, which makes readers keen to read on.

Basically, you don't want your reader to get to the end of a chapter, put the book down, walk away from it and then *not pick it up again*. What you want to create in your reader is that *'I must read one more chapter to find out what happens next'* feeling.

What is a cliff-hanger?

A cliff-hanger is a suspenseful situation occurring at the end of a chapter. Think about your favourite television series. If the series has an overarching story, you will find that there are cliff-hangers at the end of each episode or series to make sure you watch the next one. Will Rachel end up with Ross? Who killed JR? How will Buffy come back after she sacrifices herself to save Dawn? Will Picard escape the Borg?

The concept originated in the Middle Ages in a work of Arabic fiction you may be familiar with: *One Thousand and One Nights*.

In this story, Scheherazade is married to an evil king, who has a thing for marrying nice girls, spending one night with them and killing them off in the morning (clearly coffee has not been invented yet!).

Scheherazade survives by telling him stories, but she is careful to ensure that, each morning, she always stops at an exciting moment in the tale so that, if the king wants to know what happens next, he has to let her live another day.

Needless to say; she survives in this way for 1001 nights, after which point the king is in love with her and decides not to kill her after all. Her storytelling saves not only her own life, but the lives of all the girls who would have come after her. She is a storytelling hero.

The term 'cliff-hanger' was coined in 1873, when Thomas Hardy wrote *A Pair of Blue Eyes*, which had the protagonist literally hanging off a cliff.

> *Opposite Knight's eyes was an imbedded fossil, standing forth in low relief from the rock. It was a creature with eyes. The eyes, dead and turned to stone, were even now regarding him. It was one of the early crustaceans called Trilobites. Separated by millions of years in their lives, Knight and this underling seemed to have met in their place of death. It was the single instance within reach of his vision of anything that had ever been alive and had had a body to save, as he himself had now.*

Wherever you can, end your chapter on a cliff-hanger and this will increase pace and tension.

Tension

I'm talking about pacing and tension *here*, because this is the point of in the story when I have seen many adult writers struggle. They get through the introduction and inciting incident, writing exciting action, and then ... they falter. They lose impetus. The story starts to meander.

The graph below shows two stories (with 8 events in each). The story is plotted according to how tense each event is. Both stories have high points of tension (going up to a full 1 - most tense - in the climax) and also low points of tension.

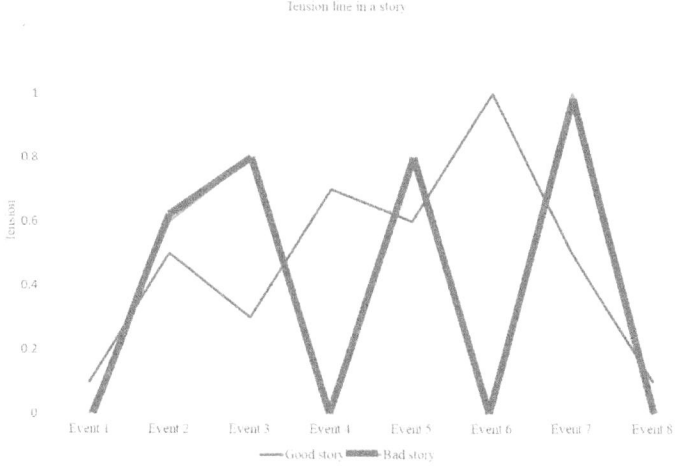

First of all, you will notice that the 'good story' – the lighter line - never drops down to zero tension. It starts (with the first event) with something a little bit exciting, and the tension builds from there. You can see where the climax is (the highest point of the line) and where the resolution is (the tension drops again at the end).

You will also notice the different shapes of the lines. The lighter line is more of a mountain shape. There are dips in the line, (moments of lower tension) but you are always climbing. The reader is permitted to take a breath, but not to completely relax.

The heavy line (the 'bad story') is more like a series of different mountains. You go from zero-tension, to high-tension, to zero-tension, to high-tension again.

Every single time the heavy line drops to zero, the author has killed the tension in the story and has to build it up from nothing again. Every time the heavy line drops to zero, this author risks losing their reader.

Notice that the line in the good story does have those lower points on the upward slope of the mountain.

Here is another graph that compares the 'good story' with another kind of 'bad story'.

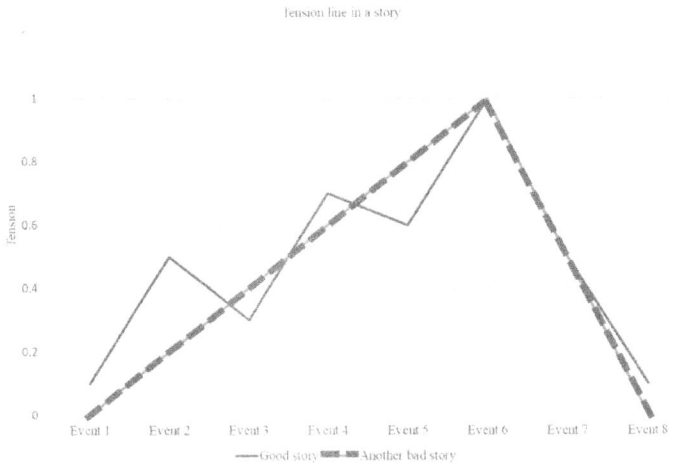

Here the tension in the 'bad story' (shown with the heavy dashed line) does nothing *but* climb, until it reaches the climax. You might think this would be an awesome story full of adventure and crisis, but you have to give your reader time to breathe, otherwise they get numb. Non-stop peril actually gets boring after a while. It is unsustainable.

Imagine your readers running through the forest pursued by a bear.

	Good story	Bad story 1	Bad story 2
1	They disturb the bear	They disturb the bear	They disturb the bear
2	They run until they are tired then hide behind a tree.	They run away and hide behind a tree.	They run away and hide behind a tree.
3	They take a moment to catch their breath - have they lost the bear?	They have a picnic. Luckily someone has brought sandwiches and ginger beer. What a lovely break!	But the bear immediately finds them. They try to climb the tree.
4	NO! It has found them. They run further and faster until they find a cave.	Oh no, the smell of food has attracted the bear again. They run away and find a cave.	Bears can climb tree! They climb to the top of the tree, but their weight makes the branches snap and they fall.
5	They take a moment to catch their breath and discuss how they might fight the bear.	Luckily someone brought a pack of cards. They sit around a campfire in the cave and play rummy – what a lovely break!	They jump from the broken tree branches, while the bear roars. They spot a cave and run towards it.
6	Oh no! They are not alone in the cave! A tiger leaps out and chases them. All looks lost until they remember that bears do not get on well with tigers! They run back towards the bear, chased by the tiger!	When, YIKES, there is a tiger in the cave. It bursts out and attacks them and they only just escape.	But, oh no, a tiger emerges from the cave and tries to eat them. There is a great battle between the tiger and bear, and they are trapped in the middle.
7	The tiger and the bear battle. This allows them to escape.	They end up back at their picnic site where they throw cans of ginger beer at the tiger and bear until they both go away.	Fighting their way free, they escape and run home, never stopping for breath.
8	They go home with a great story about their adventure in the wood.	They go home with a great story about their adventure in the wood.	They have a great story about their adventure in the wood.

Can you see how the good story allows little pauses, but the tension remains high, it is never killed off (the characters are still thinking about the bear, talking about the bear and how they might solve their problem), and when the action continues, the tension gets higher each time? While 'Bad story 1' kills off all the tension every time the characters take a break and 'Bad story 2' doesn't let up, doesn't give the reader time to breathe, or the characters time to take stock?

These *little breaks* are important. It is in these little breaks that the characters have a chance to think about what has happened, what might happen next and to plan their next course of action. It is here that your characters will reflect on the meaning of what has happened to them, and it is here that relationships will develop.

It is here that you do your character-building work, here that your characters can argue, or fall in love.

Ways to create tension – Conflict and Setting

Now that we all agree that tension is important (as well as moments of pause and reflection), how can you increase the tension in your story?

This is where **conflict** is essential. Conflict in a story is a struggle between opposing forces. It is what drives your story forward.

Without conflict, your story is going to be really dull.

There are different types of conflict:

1. **Internal** – internal or emotional obstacles (your character is at war with herself, perhaps she thinks that she isn't good enough, brave enough, strong enough, doesn't deserve love etc – and she has to defeat her own demons in order to save the day. Or perhaps your character has a moral or philosophical conflict that she has to overcome before she can triumph). *Hamlet* is a good example here – he is paralysed with indecision. His biggest obstacle to success is himself.

2. **External** - obstacles a character faces in the external world (your character is at war with someone or something else).

    a. People vs. people (Harry vs. Voldemort)

    b. People vs. society (in *Windrunner's Daughter* Wren is battling against a patriarchy that wants to keep her confined to the home)

    c. People vs. nature (*Touching the Void* is a story of adventure and endurance in the Peruvian Andes)

    d. People vs. fate (*Romeo and Juliet*)

You've probably already decided what your key conflict is going to be because you have already planned your story but, in addition to this, one of my key writing rules is:

NEVER LET YOUR PROTAGONIST HAVE IT EASY!

If there is any possible way of creating a problem for your protagonist, then create a problem. And I mean *all the time*.

If they're walking down the street, trip them up. If they are running late for a dance class, then have their car break down. If they are going somewhere with a friend, they should have an argument and so on.

Constantly create problems that they have to solve.

Even in the midst of the adventure, during the pauses for reflection, you can keep the tension from dropping to zero by adding layers of conflict. Perhaps your characters are camping in a cage for the night, having trekked through the mountains all day, while pursued by evil wizards. They are temporarily safe.

But now your main character could spill coffee on his clothes, meaning they will be wet tomorrow. He could have an argument with his friend about the best way forward. He could go outside and narrowly miss being crushed by a falling rock, which has now blocked their path onward. He could walk further into the cave and get trapped in a narrow fissure, or come face-to-face with a lion.

The other aspect of this is that you should never give them an easy time when they are facing a problem. For example, your character might be exhausted from walking. He can go no further. He needs transportation, or his quest will fail.

Which of these two options makes for a better story?

Option 1	Option 2
Your tired character stumbles on a stable. The kind farmer offers him a horse for free, because he likes his face.	Your tired character stumbles on a stable. The farmer is beating a horse. He asks if he can take the horse, as the farmer hates it so much, but the farmer laughs in his face. Your character creates a distraction by setting a small fire. The fire grows out of control, and he is almost burned. The farmer releases all of his horses to save them. Your character steals the nearest horse, and it turns out to be the horse the farmer was beating. The farmer sees him and gives chase. The beaten horse is injured and cannot fun fast enough. The farmer is almost upon him when he has to turn back to save his burning farm. Your character escapes with the horse.

Keep creating problems, little ones and big ones, that your protagonist has to solve. Never give them an easy way out of a situation.

Another way to add to tension is with **setting**.

Use the **weather** – it could be raining, a storm could be coming, the wind could be rising, or if your characters are at sea they could be becalmed or, if in the desert, getting hotter.

Use the **time of day** – it could be getting dark (or light, if they are e.g. thieves wanting to avoid discovery).

Use a **deadline** – perhaps your character needs to complete her quest before e.g. 'the sun sets three times'.

Onward (Pixar) is a good example of this - Barley and Ian have to find the Phoenix Gem to complete the spell to bring their father back for a day before the sun has set. Ian wears a watch which constantly reminds them how little time they have left.

Use the **landscape** – you could have a mountain to climb, a rockfall to bypass, a river to cross, a gorge to traverse, lava to escape, a desert to survive etc.

Scenes as building blocks

Each of your chapters will likely consist of scenes.

A scene is a sequence of events where a character, or characters, engage in some sort of action and / or dialogue. Scenes should have a beginning, a middle and an end (a mini-story), and should *move the story forward*.

When writing, every single scene must have a purpose and move the main plot on, otherwise it should be removed.

Imagine writing your story, as if you are building a tower of blocks.

Each block contributes to the height of the tower. Each block sits on the previous one, it depends on it. If any of the blocks are removed, the whole tower will fall. The climax cannot be reached.

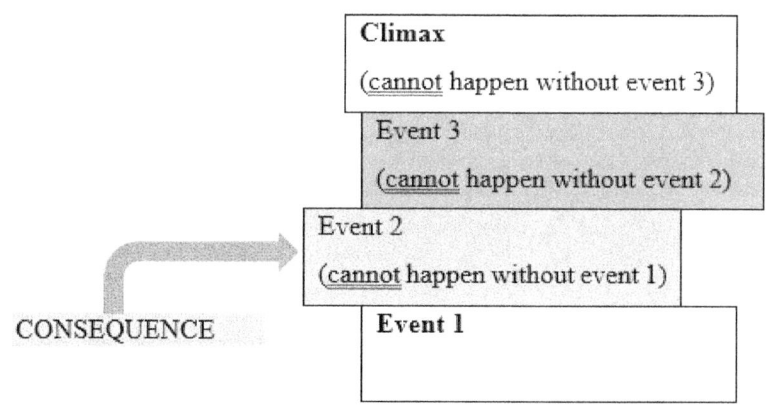

175

In other words, each scene is a CONSEQUENCE of the events of the scenes before it.

This *also* means that if you have a scene that does NOT contribute to the stability of the tower (i.e. which does *not* move the story on, or contain essential information on character or events), which can be slipped out (like a Jenga brick) without effecting the climax of the story, then it *should be removed*. Or it will kill your story off.

There are only two reasons to include a scene in your story. Either it moves the story forward, or it gives your readers essential character information (preferably both).

Before you write your scene ask yourself:
1. Does this scene move the story on?
2. Does it contain essential information on my character/s?
3. Do later scenes depend on the events of this scene?

If your answer to each question is yes, then write the scene! If the answer to any of these questions is no, then rethink its inclusion in the story.

Endings

So, you have defeated writer's block, written your opening, and completed the middle part of your story, you have kept the tension at the right level, included little breaks (which nevertheless contain some conflict), each scene builds on the one before, the climax has happened and now you're at the ending.

You've already kept your reader's interest this far, so they're going to read the ending, no matter how bad it is. So, it doesn't matter if it isn't perfect … right?

Wrong!

When you get near the ending of your book there is a huge temptation to rush. The finishing line is *in sight.* You are winning!

Now you want this race to be *over.* You *CANNOT WAIT*, to write 'The End'.

So many writers, with otherwise great stories, let themselves down at the end by rushing to get to those last two precious words.

However, ending your story is just as important as opening it so, tempting as it is, Do. Not. Rush.

Imagine you are eating your dinner – the taste of the last mouthful is the one that will stay with you all evening. Perhaps you are like my husband, who saves his best chip, or a mouthful of his favourite bit till last, because he knows that way, he'll end the meal happily.

The ending of your story is that last mouthful – it is what the reader will be left with. And if it tastes horrible, if it is disappointing or unfulfilling, then it will ruin the rest of the story.

You want your reader to pick up your next book, don't you? Then you need to leave them wanting more, not wishing they'd never even heard of you!

A great ending will stay with your reader long after they've closed the book.

A satisfying ending will **wrap up the central conflict** laid out at the start of the novel – the protagonist has achieved their goal. The reader should walk away feeling that the story is complete.

It should **answer all the unresolved questions** and **tie up the sub-plots**.

It should also **bring a close to your character development** and illustrate the transformation of the main character as a result of learning the lessons taught by the events of the story.

Great endings also **evoke emotions**. If you can leave your reader sniffing (happily or sadly) as they close the book, then they will remember your story.

My daughter just read *A Court of Silver Flames*, she read the whole thing in a day (which suggests that it was an excellent read), and the described the ending as '*low-key heart-breaking*'. She is already planning on reading it again next week!

This is as true for series fiction as it is for a standalone story.

In a series, the 'big bad' will probably not have been defeated at the end of book one, however, the story of *this part* of the adventure needs to be tied up.

Think about Harry Potter. In *Harry Potter and the Philosopher's Stone,* Harry has to defeat Professor Quirrell. We are aware that this defeat is just one step on the long road to taking down Voldemort, but he manages to win *this battle* and then return home to his aunt and uncle a changed boy, so the book feels complete, even if the over-arching story is not.

Last lines

Spend as much time thinking about the last line of your novel, as you did about your first.

Here are some famous endings to novels:

But I reckon I got to light out for the Territory ahead of the rest, because Aunt Sally she's going to adopt me and sivilize me and I can't stand it. I been there before. (Huckleberry Finn)

He was soon borne away by the waves and lost in darkness and distance. (Frankenstein)

It is a far, far better thing that I do, than I have ever done; it is a far, far better place that I go to than I have ever known. (A Tale of Two Cities)

Some of my own endings:

For at least one day, the curse could wait. (The Weight of Souls)

He walked towards me, smiling. (Savage Island)

It was the turn of the Phoenix to rise. (Phoenix Rising)

They were pirates, they had today. Tomorrow would take care of itself. (Phoenix Burning)

Like openings, let your closing line make a statement in a strong voice. If possible, refer back to your opening. Circularity is satisfying.

Writing techniques

Laying out your work like a professional

I know you have discovered that MS Word has a lot of different exciting fonts and I know that you consider *Times New Roman* the most boring of all the fonts.

But *Times New Roman* is the font most commonly used by professional writers and is therefore the font I'm going to tell you that should use. Sorry.

This is because editors expect it. It is easy for them to read. It doesn't make a statement about the writer, or the writing. Editors automatically know how long your document will be, how many words on a page and so on. It makes you *comparable*.

The last thing you want to be doing is giving your editor a headache because you've decided to start writing in ALGERIAN, Bodoni M Condensed, *Magneto*, Broadway or ◆〕■ Ŋ ♎〕■ Ŋ ◆ ⌨

Former editor, Porter tells us that he is put off submissions (that's what it's called when you send your work to an agent or publisher) printed in "*anything silly, jazzy, medieval, comic, too small, too large*", and suggests a golden rule: "*The font should never shout louder than the work.*"

There is a reason that *Times New Roman* is the industry standard – it is generally considered the easiest on tired eyes (and your agent or publisher will have tired eyes – they read a LOT). This is because it has serifs (the fiddly bits of the letter on the next page circled in red).

Serif typefaces have historically been credited with increasing both the readability and reading speed of long passages of text because they help the eye travel across a line, especially if lines are long or have relatively open word spacing (as with some justified type).

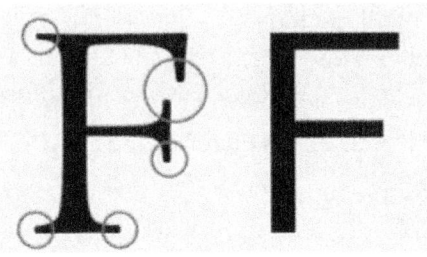

But there are other type faces with serifs so why *Times New Roman*?

Times New Roman was one of the very first typefaces created. It gets its name from the *Times of London* (the newspaper). In 1929, the *Times* hired a typographer to create a new text font and he created *Times New Roman*. Because it was used in a daily newspaper, the new font quickly became popular among printers of the day. Basically, it's been around for a really long time, and it is therefore familiar.

Now we've agreed on a font, what size should it be? I know you think the bigger the better, that way it looks like you're writing more pages, which can be satisfying. But again, there is an industry standard and that is 12-point font. Anything smaller becomes harder to read, anything bigger looks a bit … silly.

One bit of good news for you, is that your work should be laid out using double-line spacing (there you go, that makes for a lot of nice white space on the page). Again, it eases your reader's tired eyes, and when editors are making notes on print outs (some still do this) it gave enough space for scribblings between lines.

In conclusion, to write a professional looking document you should use:

Times New Roman, 12-point size, double-line spacing.

Each page should also be **numbered** (most publishers prefer numbering at the bottom of the page).

Your document should also have a **header**, including both your name and the title of your book, this means that if an editor has printed out a number of manuscripts and loses a page from yours, he or she can easily find the correct place to reinsert it.

Your story should, of course, also have a **title page.** This should include your title, (centralised and written in a larger font), your name, your word count, the genre (more on that later) and target audience (more on that later too). Then you should include your contact details so you can be offered a book deal very easily.

When writing the story itself, you need to make sure that **new paragraphs**, including new dialogue, are indicated with a *single* carriage return, and indented.

A *double* carriage return is only used to show a **section break**, or hiatus (a gap in time).

When you begin a chapter or new section after a hiatus / section break your first sentence should *not* be indented.

Punctuation

Honestly, if you're in school you are probably better than I am at grammar and punctuation (especially with all those SPAG classes!), but I'm including this section for reference, and for those old folk (like me), for whom school was a long time ago!

Sentences

A sentence is a collection of words that conveys sense or meaning, formed according to the logic of grammar.

There are four types of sentence -

1. A **Declarative sentence**, which states a fact and ends with a full stop.

    It is raining.

2. An **Imperative sentence,** which is a command or a polite request. It ends with an exclamation mark or a full stop.

    Stand still!

3. An **Interrogative sentence**, which asks a question and ends with a question mark.

    What are you doing?

4. An **Exclamatory sentence**, which expresses excitement or emotion. It ends with an exclamation mark.

    What a brilliant piece of writing!

In an imperative sentence (an order) or an interrogative sentence (a question), the subject or verb can be implied.

Run!

Go. (This is the shortest sentence in English.)

Why?

The shortest sentence without an implied subject or verb is "I am" or "I go."

The simplest sentences contain a **noun** and a **verb** -

Catherine walked.

Most sentences have a **subject noun** and an **object noun** -

Catherine walked towards the hotel.

Catherine is the subject noun (a person or thing performing the action). The hotel is the object noun (a person or thing towards which the action is directed).

Adjectives describe nouns. They usually come before the noun (lovely)-

Lovely Catherine walked towards the old hotel.

Adverbs describe verbs (quickly).

Lovely Catherine walked quickly towards the old hotel.

When using tense, then you must remain consistent within the sentence. Decide whether you are explaining an event in the past, present or future and be consistent in that tense until there is a good reason for changing.

A **fragment** is sentence which is not complete and therefore grammatically incorrect. Sentence fragments are problematic because they are disjointed and confusing to the reader.

There are three main causes of fragments:

1. A missing subject.
2. A missing verb.
3. 'danger' words which are unfinished.

There are three ways to check for sentence completion –

1. Find the subject (the noun or pronoun about which something is written). Identify who or what is doing the action. If there is no subject, the sentence is a fragment.

2. Find the verb (the action word in the sentence). Identify what happened. If there is no identifiable action, the sentence is a fragment.

3. Check for 'danger words'. A danger word is one which introduces a thought which requires a follow-up phrase. Such words are often called cliff-hangers, because they begin a statement, but leave it hanging without a finish. Danger words include, *if, when and because.*

A run-on sentence is a sentence that contains two or more complete sentences, without the proper punctuation. There are two types. The comma-splice, where a comma is used instead of a full-stop or a lack of punctuation, where a semi-colon is needed.

Full-stops

A full stop comes at the end of a sentence. You might think this is obvious, but you'd be amazed at the number of adult writers who mis-use full-stops.

Commas

Commas customarily indicate a brief pause. They are not as final as a full stop.

You can use commas to separate words and word groups in a simple series of three or more items, for example when writing lists -

We ate sausages, eggs, chips and beans.

You can use commas to separate two adjectives when the order of the adjectives is interchangeable -

It was a hot, bright summer's day.

Another way to determine if a comma is needed is to mentally put *and* between the two adjectives. If the result still makes sense, add the comma.

In sentences where two independent clauses are joined by connectors such as *and, or, but*, etc., put a comma at the end of the first clause -

He walked all the way home, and he shut the door.

If the subject does not appear in front of the second verb, a comma is generally unnecessary.

When starting a sentence with a dependent clause, use a comma after it.

Even though the broccoli was covered in cheese, Maisie refused to eat it.

Non-essential words, clauses, and phrases that occur midsentence must be enclosed by commas. The closing comma is called an appositive comma. Many writers forget to add this important comma.

Amelie, who was walking her dog, wore her trainers to the park.

I tend to work out when I need this comma by asking myself, can that middle part of the sentence be removed, leaving a complete sentence behind it (*Amelie wore her trainers to the park*)? If the answer is yes, then you *bookend* that middle bit of the sentence with commas.

Use a comma after certain words that introduce a sentence, such as well, yes, why, hello, hey, etc.

Well, he never did like to drink coffee.

Use commas to set off expressions that interrupt the sentence flow (nevertheless, after all, by the way, on the other hand, however, etc.).

Arwen wanted to go to the park however, she had to go to work.

Use commas to set off the name, nickname, term of endearment, or title of a person directly addressed.

Yes, Mrs Pearce, I think you are indeed correct.

There are more rules here on this website, if you would like to look into it further:

http://www.grammarbook.com/punctuation/commas.asp

However, my own personal favourite rule is as follows:

If in doubt, *don't*.

Semi-colons

A semi-colon creates more separation between thoughts than a comma, but less than a full stop. The two most common uses are to join two sentences, or help separate items in a list, when some of those items already contain commas:

I bought shiny, ripe apples; small, juicy grapes; sweet, firm pears and a punnet of strawberries.

An independent clause is a group of words that can stand on its own (independently) – it is a complete sentence. Semi-colons can be used between two independent clauses, to keep the clauses separate, but suggest a close relationship between them.

I went to the woods today. I had to run all the way home; I was chased by a bear.

You could write:

I went to the woods today. I had to run all the way home. I was chased by a bear.

But you want to suggest that the *reason* you ran all the way home was the bear chasing you, so you link the sentences together with a semi-colon.

I often think of it this way – if you could write 'because', but don't want to, you could use a semi-colon.

Colons

Like the semi-colon, the colon also follows an independent clause. It can be used to present an explanation, draw attention to something or join ideas together.

You can use a colon to announce a list -

I bought a lot of vegetables at the shop: peas, potatoes, carrots and onions.

You can use a colon to announce a quotation -

Shakespeare said it best: To thine own self be true.

And to announce an example / explanation –

Many children find that there are advantages to reading for fun: strengthening test scores, escaping from reality and improving their own writing skills.

Colons can also be used to connect two sentences when the second summarizes or sharpens the first. Both sentences should be complete, and their content closely related.

Life is like a puzzle: the fun is in working it out.

Check if you are using the colon correctly, by reading the material preceding the colon and establishing whether or not it is a complete sentence that can stand on its own.

Apostrophes

An apostrophe is a punctuation mark (') used to indicate either possession (when you add an s to a regular noun)

That is Riley's book.

or the omission of letters or numbers (*can't, shan't, won't, doesn't, weren't, couldn't, shouldn't etc.*)

He can't come to the park today; he was chased by a bear last night.

She won't like that cauliflower; it doesn't have any cheese on it.

I'll be honest, though, there is one word in which even the most seasoned of writers can mis-use the apostrophe. This word is the dreaded -

IT'S

There is a bear in the wood and it's chasing us!

It's means it is or it has. The apostrophe signals that something has been removed:

It's raining. [=It is raining.]

It's been raining since last night. [=It has been raining since last night.]

Meanwhile, *its* means of or relating to it or itself:

Let the medicine do its job.

What used to confuse me is that possessive.

The car isn't working it's battery is dead. (WRONG)

I used to think that as the battery belongs to the car, then an apostrophe is required. I was wrong. So, my easy to learn rule is -

If you can replace *its* with *his* and it still makes sense, then don't use an apostrophe.

For more information on apostrophes you could look here -

www.grammarbook.com/punctuation/apostro.asp

How you can use punctuation to create a voice

Don't forget that you can have fun with punctuation. For example, you can use punctuation to help create voice. In my newest adult novel, I have written three characters and they have alternating chapters written from their own perspectives.

Kelly is a very stressed-out and unhappy woman. She uses a lot of very short sentences, where another character might use a comma, to extend a sentence, she uses a full-stop.

Aleema is a highly educated woman with a job writing articles for science magazines, her sections have long sentences, broken up with colons and semi-colons.

Naomi is not highly educated, but she is very relaxed. She too has longer sentences, but she never uses colons / semi-colons, instead she uses a dash to indicate that she is writing e.g. an explanation.

Show not tell

This one is the biggie!

All fiction writers are told to *show not tell*.

Many writers who come to me say that they know what it means, but then their writing 'shows' me that either they don't actually know what it means, or they are not applying it correctly.

Show not tell is one of *the* writing techniques that makes a writer stand out. If you can master show not tell, you'll be writing like the professionals.

But *why* are we told to show and not tell?

Well, *showing is more effective at conveying information*.

Imagine you have to set up a fishing rod. What is easier – reading instructions on how to do it, or having someone else show you how to do it?

Showing also *increases the impact* of what you are trying to say.

There's a reason that your teachers ask you to do science experiments, rather than just telling you what happens when you, for example, mix two chemicals together, or burn a peanut. It is because *letting people work something out for themselves makes it more memorable*.

So, not only is telling amateur writing, but it reduces the effectiveness of what you are trying to convey.

Which of these pieces of writing is more effective / stays with you for longer?

Option 1	Option 2
'You dirty rat!' Mike slammed his fist into the table. 'I'll never forgive you.' Tears gathered in the corners of his eyes but were burned away before they could fall. His fist trembled on the wood, and he curled his lip, wishing it was Dan's face being ground under his knuckles, but Dan was on the other end of the phone, a hundred miles away.	*During Mike's phone call, he was very angry.*

Can you see now why telling should be avoided where possible?

So, what actually *is* **show not tell**?

Picture yourself watching your favourite television programme, say *Scooby Doo*. You are nearing the end of the show and Scooby and Shaggy have encountered the ghost. Suddenly the screen goes black.

A voiceover comes on: *'The ghost jumps out at Scooby, and Scooby and Shaggy run around while the ghost chases them. Fred's trap is sprung, but does not work and Daphne gets kidnapped.'*

How would you feel about this episode? You would be pretty upset if you were watching it … right?

This is telling and not showing, the viewer has been thrown out of the show, and instead of watching the action, is being told what is happening.

When reading, many readers end up with a picture, or movie, in their heads of what is going on. This is created by you, the writer and is done by using accurate description and by showing the reader what is going on.

When you start telling, the movie in the reader's head is stopped, just like that episode of *Scooby Doo*.

Let me give you an example.

Telling a scene
The man tried to run after us, but we had darted in the other direction, determined to hide. The man looked annoyed as he strode back into the alleyway and walked away, kicking the ground as he did so.
Very little detail. Not staying with the characters and what is happening to them. Telling the reader what happened instead of showing it happening. Rushed.

Showing a scene

"Ayesha, run!"
     Our feet pounded down the alleyway as the man started to shout. "Get back here!"
     "No way, creep!" I yelled. We caught up to the panting Ayesha. "Now what?"
     "We have to hide. Quick down here." Jordyn pointed to a ginnel off the alley, filled with black plastic bins and crumpled bags. The smell of rotting rubbish was a smack in the face, but none of us complained. We dived behind the biggest of the bins, and crouched with our arms around one another. Ayesha was trembling. I tightened my grip on her.
     "It'll be okay," I whispered.
     But the man's footsteps were coming nearer.
     "Where are you?" He called. "Come out, come out wherever you are!"
     Jordyn started to sob, silently, her shoulders shaking.
     Then, suddenly there was another voice.
     "Oi, what are you doing back there?"
     We looked up. A woman was leaning from a window above us, her shoulders barely fitting through the frame. "Go on, get orf out of it."
     The man jumped, and he stopped moving closer.
     "Go on," the woman yelled. "Scarper. Or do I need to call the police?"

Lots of detail. Remaining with the characters and what is happening to them. Showing the reader what is happening. Slowing down and drilling into the moment.

Often telling creeps into writing when you are tired, rushing, or keen to get to another scene. If you find yourself skipping details, or telling, then have a break and come back to your writing later, when you are refreshed.

Other times, telling creeps in when a writer needs to give the reader *information* about character background, world history, or explain what is happening. This is called exposition (explaining) and comes across as an information dump for the reader.

Information dumping (telling)
In the olden times, the Cursed Sword was wielded by none other than Dragorn the Mighty, the great hero who defeated the evil King Frithor, saved the city and married his beautiful daughter, the Princess Ragiel. But when the magician Olvich turned up, to take over his kingdom, Dragorn had to go out to battle. With his dying breath he managed to defeat the king, but the Cursed Sword fell into a lava filled crevice and was never seen again.
Telling information in a boring way.

Showing the same information

'What's that on the map? It doesn't look like a place.'
    'Hamish is right, it looks like … a sword.'
    'Ah,' the old man sighed. 'Yes, that is the resting place of the Cursed Sword, so they say.'
    'The Cursed Sword?' Hamish leaned closer. 'Cool!'
    The old man rolled his eyes. 'Yes, cool.'
    'Why was it cursed?' Tofunmi asked, nervously. 'And why is it marked on an ordinary map?'
    The old man smiled mistily. 'That was the sword of Dragorn the Mighty,' he struck a pose, as if he was holding a sword, then sagged. 'He died defending the city against the magician Olvich and his sword was lost right about … there.'

-    Showing the same information via a scene.

If you find yourself 'info dumping' have a think about more creative ways your character (and therefore reader) can discover the information.

Could your character find old letters, or an old book or diary, that might show them the information? Could they watch an old video or home movie which contains important memories? Could they have a conversation with an old relative, or mentor? Could they find newspaper clippings, see an old photo, or sit in a history lesson at school?

In *Harry Potter,* JK Rowling gets around the problem by inventing the Pensieve, a magical device which enables Harry to see into the past as if he is right there inside the action.

In *Angel's Fury* there is a lot for the main character, Cassie, to find out, both about her own history and about the past. So she has flashbacks from other people's lives in the form of nightmares.

> *The men won't stop to let us clean up Amos' sick. It oozes into the grooves around our shoes and the smell mixes with the reek of petrol until I feel sick too. I swallow and cover my mouth.*

She watches an old home movie which shows her as a baby.

> *The screen was a magic mirror, reversing the damage of the years. In this image Dad's hair was brown, his skin unlined. But his mouth was flat above his jutting chin and he was aged by the shadows in his eyes.*

And later she discovers an ancient journal, that belongs to a fallen angel, which fills in more of the story for her.

The book was there, nested like a living thing in a mulch of felt and velvet. Just as I'd dreamed, the cover was black with age and the scaled binding was tough and brittle at the edges. It did not completely overlap all of the rough pages, which protruded like a mass of tongues. I brushed my palm over the cover and recoiled. The leather was slippery and organic.

I've already mentioned that I avoided lots of exposition in *Phoenix Rising*, by using a mish-mash of newspaper articles. You can be as creative as you like, just as long as you avoid telling.

Another form of telling is that of telling the reader how your character is feeling.

Telling emotion	Showing emotion
'I really don't like it,' Amina said, sadly.	Amina dashed a tear from her eye. 'I really don't like it.'

When I am writing, I will often stop what I am doing, pull funny faces, walk around the room, curl up in a ball or clench my fists. What I am trying to do, is put myself in the place of my character and work out how they are *acting* in a way that corresponds to how they are *feeling*.

If my character is terrified, I think back to a time when I was really scared, and then imagine myself there. How am I feeling? What am I doing with my body? Am I cold, or hot? Are my fists clenched, or open? Have I frozen, am I running away, or looking for somewhere to hide? Am I frowning? Is my face screwed up? Am I screaming, or is my mouth in a flat line? Am I preparing to fight, or run? Am I shivering? Am I holding my hands in front of my face?

That way when my character is frightened, I can show them being frightened in a realistic way that readers will recognise, and I won't need to tell them that she is frightened.

Writing Exercise

Write a list of emotions. For example: Grief, Rage, Anxiety, Fear, Excitement, Embarrassment, Affection, Happiness, Hatred.
Then take each emotion one at a time and explore them in depth.

I will use rage as an example. Try and think of a time in your life when you have truly felt angry. Close your eyes and take yourself back in your own mind. Remember how you really felt. Write a short piece describing the event - what did you see, feel, taste, hear, smell? Go into as much detail as possible: Did you get hot? Did the heat arrive instantly, or did it build slowly? Where did the heat come from? Did you literally see red? Did you lose control - in what way? Were your fists clenched? What about your toes? What happened to your face? Did it screw up or stretch out? Did your muscles tense? Did you shake? Were your other senses affected - did you taste or smell anything as a result of your rage? How were you moving - fast and jerky or slow and deliberate? Did you run, walk, crawl? How did you wrestle yourself back into control? How did you feel afterwards? Shaky, exhausted, embarrassed, proud, relieved?

Once you have done this for a range of emotions you will have a list of physical descriptions that you can use in your novel to help you signpost consistently how your characters are feeling.

The gap

This form of showing works because people have life experience. If your character is crying, your reader will know she is sad. If your character is smiling, your reader will know he is happy and so on.

This also works with other things. If you show that it is clouding over, your reader knows it is going to rain, if your protagonist hears a siren, your reader knows that an emergency vehicle is on the way.

This is called 'the gap'.

	GAP	
Ben hung his head and a tear fell onto his shoe	… so therefore	he is upset
Abigail stamped her foot. 'I hate you.'	… so therefore	
Rohan looked at the time and his shoulders slumped 'Oh … I missed it,' he said.	… so therefore	
The mountain was covered in snow, and there was a deep, terrifying rumbling	… so therefore	
The sun was low in the sky	… so therefore	
Smoke started to emerge from the top of the volcano	… so therefore	

The older your reader is, the more life experience they have and the wider the gap you can leave between what you are showing and what you want them to work out for themselves.

In a book for adults, you can be very subtle in showing how one character feels about another, for example. Perhaps if one character is in love with another, she might always bring him a coffee in the morning made just the way he likes it and that would be enough to signal her feelings to the reader.

As your reader gets younger, they have less life experience and it is harder for them to work out, from subtle signals, what is going on. This means that the gap between showing and telling has to get smaller.

Take, as an example, the sun setting -

Adult book	Young adult book	Mid-grade book	Early reader
'Shepherd's delight' I thought, glancing at the sky with a smile.	Dragorn's armour caught the light and glinted red as if it were on fire.	The sun was low behind the trees and the sky was red.	The sun was setting.

Something very clever that Mark Haddon does in The *Curious Incident of the Dog in the Night-time*, is he writes a main character who does not have much life experience and who requires a near non-existent gap in order to know what is going on. However, Haddon knows that his reader has more life experience than his character. This means that, although the story is told in limited perspective, the reader often knows more about what is going on than the main character, because we understand things that he does not.

One final exercise to make sure that you have got the hang of show not tell. Change each of the following examples of telling, into showing instead.

Writing exercise	
Mark was excited that he had been asked to join the football team.	
Dylan was sad that he had missed the show.	
Vaughan was angry with Daniel	
Saira was embarrassed that her lie had been uncovered.	
Mansoor was happy to be invited to the party.	
The volcano was about to erupt.	
The house was on fire.	
The wizard was about to cast a deadly spell.	

Passive vs active voice

Now you know about show not tell, your writing will appear professional, but there are a few other traps that amateur writers can fall into and that you must avoid. One of these traps is passive voice.

You need to avoid passive voice because it distances your reader from the action and slows things down. Active voice puts the reader right into the action and is therefore best, especially if you are writing a tense adventure story.

The active voice emphasizes the person or agent who performs an action, in short, the "actor." The passive voice emphasizes the recipient of the action or sometimes the action itself.

Active voice	Passive voice
The football player kicked the ball.	The ball was kicked by the football player.
Here the football player is the star of the sentence. The sentence is concise (shorter). More direct. Stronger.	Here the ball is the star of the sentence. The sentence is unnecessarily wordy and clunky.

How to tell if you are using passive voice:

1. You use too many 'be-verbs' (was, were, are, etc.).

2. You write 'realised' or 'felt'.

3. You are treating body parts as if they're separate from the person.

Active voice	Passive voice
The dog chased the ball.	The ball was chased by the dog
I felt exhausted.	I was exhausted.
I realised that it was getting dark.	It was getting dark.
My body ached all over.	I ached all over.
Her eyes looked from left to right and her feet started to run.	She looked from left to right and started to run.

Writing Exercise
Find your last piece of creative writing, search for all instances of the words felt and realised. Remove them from the writing. See how much more effective your writing becomes.

Excellent description

When I read a good book, I can see what is happening in my head, like watching a film. Does that happen for you?

When I can do that, it is because the writer has described what is going on in their story very well. In particular, they have described their characters so that I can picture them living the events of the story.

There are ways of describing however, that are very effective and ways that are less effective.

Hunting and killing adverbs and adjectives

"When you catch an adjective, kill it. No, I don't mean utterly, but kill most of them—then the rest will be valuable. They weaken when they are close together. They give strength when they are wide apart." Mark Twain

Many writers like to use adverbs and adjectives to add to their descriptions.

*When the **lovely, bouncy** music stopped, I walked **quickly** towards the **old, filthy, red** chair.*

This is perfectly accurate, and for a certain level of writing, fine. Your teachers probably love a good adjective (in my son's primary school they were called *WOW! Words* and I've seen teachers go pale when I suggest that creative writers cut them from their work)!

However, piles of adjectives actually slow your writing down (remember how important pacing is) and can even make writing difficult to read and understand. I've been sent writing by adult writers that I've had to reread several times to get the meaning, just because so many adjectives were used in a paragraph.

This is how a professional writer might describe the same situation (above).

The music stopped and I sped towards the chair. It was older than my nan, and layers of dirt made it almost impossible to tell that, once upon a time, it had been as red as the dress I was wearing.

Can you see that I have described the same thing (walking quickly towards the old, filthy, red chair), but have not used one single adverb or adjective. Mine is easier to read and understand, and I've also managed to include a lot more detail. They are obviously playing musical chairs, the character has an elderly grandmother, she is wearing a red dress.

Here are two writing samples:

Writing sample one (lots of adjectives and adverbs)
The **tall** girl in the **shimmering blue** swimsuit dived **gracefully** into the **bright blue** lake and vanished, leaving **giant** ripples that shivered across the **iridescent** water and **quickly** disappeared in their turn leaving behind no sign of her **elegant** presence.

Writing sample two (one adverb)
Emma prepared to dive, lifting her arms over her head and enjoying her stretch. The sun caught her swimsuit, turning her torso into the body of a kingfisher, feathered with snatches of light. Even though the lake was opaque as foil, she dived with no hesitation, slicing through the water like a blade to leave behind only a few ripples that vanished as **quickly** as she.

Which piece of writing do you think is better in terms of description?

Some people genuinely do prefer sample one. But most find sample two much more evocative and informative and it proves that you can write descriptive passages without overloading with adverbs / adjectives.

Proviso

This doesn't mean you should *never* use adjectives. Sometimes the right adjective can truly sparkle in a piece of description, but if there are too many, the reader is dazzled. Imagine it like this.

You are a jeweller, and you have the most perfect diamond. Its clarity is unsurpassed, the cut is perfect. You want to display it for a customer. You choose a piece of dark blue velvet, you put the diamond in the centre of the velvet. How does that look?

Then you chuck a handful of cubic zirconia around the diamond. Now does it stand out?

Think of your adjectives like that diamond. Choose your single most perfect one, perhaps two if you really must. You may use that on a page, but no more. The rest of that page is your velvet cloth, do not sprinkle other inferior jewels over that cloth.

Read some of your favourite writers. Spend some time counting the number of adverbs and adjectives they use in a single page. You will be surprised how few you find.

Writing Exercise
Try removing all but one of the adverbs and adjectives on each of your pages of creative writing. Then read it out loud. You'll be amazed at how much better it sounds.

But if most of your adjectives and adverbs have to be removed, what can you use instead?

When considering replacing an adverb ask yourself if you can find a more effective verb. For example, instead of 'run quickly', why not write 'sprinted', ''dashed or ''raced? Instead of 'walk slowly', why not write 'ambled', 'meandered' or 'wandered'?

When considering replacing adjectives in descriptions there are a number of different techniques that you could use.

Let's look at the writing samples I showed you earlier. What alternative techniques did I use to describe the same situation?

The **tall** girl	Sensory description	Emma prepared to dive, lifting her arms over her head and enjoying her stretch.
... the **shimmering blue** swimsuit	Metaphor	The sun caught her swimsuit, turning her torso into the body of a kingfisher, feathered with snatches of light.
the **iridescent** water	Simile	Even though the lake was opaque as foil.
dived **gracefully** into the **bright blue** lake	Simile	slicing through the water like a blade

Simile

Simile is something you likely will have already learned in school. Simile is when you compare one thing to another by saying that something is LIKE something else.

Examples of similes
She was as tired as a teacher after a lesson with class 7R.
The fire engine was as red as the spot on the end of Megan's nose.
The night was as dark as the inside of a suitcase.
He hissed like a snake.

If you use 'like' or 'as', you are using a simile.

Now you try writing some:

Writing exercise
The pond was flat like a
The fire was as hot as
Mum was as angry as
The teacher was as kind as

Simile is a very effective form of description, especially if you are describing something or someone that your reader is not very familiar with. Comparing it with something the reader *is* familiar with, enables them to more clearly see the thing you are describing.

Like the adjectives, however, don't load up too many, otherwise your pacing will slow right down. One or two per paragraph is probably enough.

Metaphor

Metaphor is similar to simile, but it is levelled up. Instead of saying that one thing is LIKE another, with metaphor, you say that one thing IS another thing.

My teacher is a teddy-bear.

Uncle Andrew is the black sheep of the family.

All the world's a stage, and all the men and women merely players.

Metaphor is stronger than simile and can be really effective. But used wrongly it can be a little odd, so use carefully, as if you had a jar of tabasco in your hand and were adding to your meal!

Now you try.

Writing exercise	
Redescribe each of these things using metaphor -	
The red car is a ...	
The fish in the pond is a ...	
The excited boy is a ...	
The angry teacher is a ...	
The goldfish in the bowl is a ...	

There are also more subtle forms of metaphor that you can use.

Implied metaphor

This allows you to make a sophisticated comparison via implication.

Mohammed's feathers were ruffled.

This suggests to the reader that Mohammed is annoyed, because when a bird is disturbed it ruffles its feathers. I do not say that Mohammed *is* a bird, but I am saying that he has feathers, which *implies* that Mohammed is a bird: *implied metaphor.*

The baby squawked for food.

Again, it is birds that squawk, so I am analogising the baby human to a baby bird.

Sustained metaphor

Another form of metaphor that is particularly powerful is *sustained metaphor*. This is where you give us a metaphor once, but then *don't let it go*. This can go on for a whole paragraph, or even longer, for a whole chapter, or a whole story:

But soft! What light through yonder window breaks? It is the East, and Juliet is the sun! Arise, fair sun, and kill the envious moon, who is already sick and pale with grief.

Here Shakespeare is telling us that Romeo thinks of Juliet as the sun. He compares her to a light.

What light through yonder window breaks? (What light (Juliet) is coming through that window over there?)

He calls the window the East – which is where the sun rises.

It is the East.

He then literally calls Juliet the sun.

and Juliet is the sun.

If Juliet is the sun, we know that everything from now in the story will revolve around her. The sun brings life, but too strong, too hot and it brings death. Think of the tale of Icarus who got too close to the sun – what happened to him? Romeo is about to get too close to the sun!

He tells her to rise (like the sun).

Arise, fair sun,

And finishes with a suggestion that she kill (replace) the moon (*and kill the envious moon, who is already sick and pale with grief*), which is jealous of her beauty.

This extends the metaphor, is likely also a reference to Romeo's old love, Rosaline, who Juliet has replaced in his affection *and* is probably also a reference to the Roman goddess of the moon (Diana) who is the protectress of virgins. Romeo wants Juliet to cast off her virginity to be with him (Shakespeare is *dead clever* isn't he!).

Shakespeare extends this metaphor of Juliet being a source of great light, by describing her as such elsewhere (via implied metaphor).

She doth teach the torches to burn bright!

Suppose you have a character who is hard-hearted and emotionless, you could perhaps describe them like a robot early on.

She smiled, robotically.

Every time you move to this character you could think about extending this metaphor.

Her skin was shiny like it had been oiled and her eyes seemed to see through you, red lights in her expressionless face. She acted with small jerky movements, as if she was thinking carefully about each gesture before making it.

She was titanium.

Her phone, which always seemed a part of her, beeped loudly, making us jump.

Dead metaphor

When you are writing metaphors, however, do make sure that you think of *original* ideas - things that you haven't heard before.

A living metaphor is one that makes us think. That description of the woman above as a robot brought an image into your mind because it made you stop and consider it.

A dead metaphor has been over-used so much that we no longer even think about the image.

It's raining cats and dogs.

He had a heart of gold.

It's brass monkeys out there.

A tower of strength.

Publishers are looking for unique voices, using dead metaphors will make an editor think that you don't have anything to say for *yourself.*

Mixed metaphor

Also be very careful about mixing your metaphors. A mixed metaphor is when you start comparing the thing you are describing as one thing, and then slip into comparing it as something else.

All at once, he was alone in this noisy hive with no place to roost.

The new job has allowed her to spread her wings and really blossom.

You can use mixed metaphors if you're trying to be funny, otherwise avoid them.

The Window

Using simile and metaphor to add to characterisation

One of the exciting things about simile and metaphor is that they can be looked through in two directions, like a pane of glass.

Adrian's feet smelled like Gran's three-day-old liver and onions.

Looked through one way this tells us that Adrian's feet are *really* stinky.

Looked through the other direction, this tells us that your speaker has a gran, who makes liver and onions and leaves it lying around for three days, and that the speaker finds this really disgusting and stinky.

In fact, this simile tells us more about the speaker and her life than it does about Adrian. About Adrian, we know that he has smelly feet. About the speaker we know that she has a gran, who is a bad cook, who leaves disgusting food lying around for days and feeds it to the speaker.

So, when you are coming up with metaphors and similes, you need to think hard about who is speaking. Who is narrating your story?

Most of the time it won't be *your* voice (unless you are writing an autobiography, a diary, or a character who is 100% based on yourself).

Assuming you are not writing autobiographically, you must try and come up with similes and metaphors not that *you* would come up with, but that *your character* would come up with.

Imagine a character living in a fantasy world, like Middle Earth (TLOTR). There is a great rumbling sound.

How would this character describe this rumbling?

Rumbling like an engine.
Rumbling like drums on a feast day.

This character has never heard an engine, so how could he describe the rumbling as '*like an engine*'?

So, when you are writing description, don't just think about *what* you are describing, think about the character who is *doing* the describing.

Are they, for example, a builder, a teacher, an artist, an engineer, a dancer, a scientist etc? Where do they live? What life experience do they have? How would they see the world?

Take, for example, a building. How would these different people describe this one thing?

Engineer	An engineer might look at how the building is put together, the materials, the angles, whether it is safe or not.
Politician	A politician might think in terms of how the residents might vote, whether the building needs changing / improving for his constituency, who might live here and how they can help him.
Dancer	A dancer might think in terms of flow, space, music.
Artist	An artist might think about colour, shape and light.
Film director	A film director might think in terms of frames, scenes, what could happen where.

Writing exercise

Find a picture of a building. Describe it three times, in three different ways - from the point of view of an engineer, a politician and an artist.

Think about what *they* would see when looking at the building, what metaphors and similes *they* would use.

Can you see how describing the same thing from these different perspectives shows the reader as much about the character speaking and what is important to *them*, as about the thing being described?

Writing as if you're really there - Sensory Description

Now we've talked about metaphor and simile, there is another way of describing things which is very effective and quite easy to do, once you are aware that you need to do it. This is describing using *all five* of your senses (sensory description).

Sometimes writers send me work and I notice is that it all feels very 'top level', I am not being drawn into the scene. This is usually because they are only showing me what their character can *see* and are missing out all of the other things that character can sense. What do they smell, hear, taste and feel? If I don't get shown this, then I'm unlikely to feel immersed in the scene.

Consider a description of say, a rainforest. There are five levels on which this could work:

Level one: Sight

I am surrounded by trees with vines as thick as my arm snaking up them. Canopies of leaves blot out the sky and there are flashes of colour among the green – red flowers, rainbow-coloured birds and brown monkeys with bruised-looking bottoms.

You could leave your description there of course, but are you, as reader, really there with me? No, it's like looking at a picture. So, add sound.

Level two: 2. Sound:

The monkeys chatter like a class of primary school kids on an outing, their teeth flashing as they squeal and bounce on the tree branches. Bird song weaves in and out of the vines, sharp and high, or low and sonorous. A distant howl rolls through the air.

You, as a reader are now more present. It is like watching a film, rather than just looking at a static picture; but you could get closer. We can make our experience three-dimensional and add smell.

Level three: Smell

I sniff and the heady scent of flowers lifts me forward as if I am in a dream, I am a bee drawn towards the sticky stamens. But underneath it all, the scent of rot: rotting leaves beneath my feet, bones mouldering under tree roots and my own sweat, drying under my arms and on my back.

We are now close to the picture, our noses pressed against the screen, but we could get closer still. Add touch to really get into the character's experience.

Level four: touch

My clothes stick to me, clammy cotton on my spine, khaki chafing my thighs. as my feet crunch and shush through the mulch. Dangling vines tangle in the kinks of my hair and my fingers snarl in the gluey yarn of a cobweb. I gasp as something tickles my palm, running lightly over my skin, a hundred legs, and gone. My skin is wet, the humid air drowning me in dampness, heat in my eyes, up my nose, coating my lungs until every exhalation is wet and my lips are cracked.

Finally, to get completely into the character and the experience, to put the reader inside the character, add taste. Unless the character is eating a meal, this can be the hardest sense to use.

Level five: taste

On the back of my tongue the smell of decomposition has turned to copper and mould: meaty and slick. I can taste the air, hot and humid sliding down my throat like wine. The lunch I had is still with me, seeds in my teeth, banana on my breath.

Can you see how, by the final phrase, you have engaged completely with this character; you are there with her in the rainforest, not only seeing what she does, but experiencing with her? If you never get past the first couple of levels, you aren't taking your reader with you.

Writing exercise
Where are you sitting? Look around. Now describe this place using all five of your senses. See how far down the levels you can get.
Can you see how effective this description is, compared to a description that only uses what you can see?

Other things to do

There are a few other tricks that professional writers use. Little rules that help us to write really well.

1. <u>Avoid repetition.</u>

Repetition annoys readers and there are different forms of it.

Repetition of information – you need to trust your reader to remember important things that have happened in your story. You are not making a presentation to a bunch of bored businessmen or teaching a lesson. You *don't* need to tell the reader what you are going to tell them, tell it and then tell them what you told them (which is the rule for presenting by the way). Your reader isn't your student, you just need to show them something once. If you've written your scene effectively enough, it will remain with the reader, and there will be no need to show them *again*. There is nothing more irritating then reading a chapter which begins with a recap of what happened in the last chapter (whether through the character thinking about it, dreaming of it, or discussing it).

Repetition of phrases – I know you've come up with a great phrase or wow word! You want to use it over-and-over again, to show how clever you are. *But you mustn't!* Use it only once. In fact, the cleverer your word or phrase is, the more it will stick in the reader's mind and the more obvious the repetition will be if you reuse it. The cleverer something is, in fact, the *less* you should reuse it.

Repetition of words – This is the hardest one to avoid, basically it means do not use the same word more than once within a few lines (preferably on a page). Now, I'm not talking about the words you have to use a lot like conjunctions (the, and, as, a etc), I'm talking about other words.

Look at this piece of writing:

'Please be seated,' the teacher said.

I sat on my seat. It wasn't very comfortable. In fact, the seat was made of hard plastic and there was a bit of splintered wood on the back of the seat that was digging into my back like the spine of a hedgehog.

'What's wrong with you, Sophie?' The teacher asked as I wriggled in my seat. 'Is there something wrong with your seat?'

It's pretty awful isn't it?

There is nothing wrong with it per se – I use a nice simile, the dialogue evokes the speaker, it's laid out correctly, I use a bit of sensory description, my dialogue tags are appropriate. However, I use the word 'seat' a total of six times! That is what makes it bad. You knew it was bad when you were reading it. Perhaps it even made you laugh. So, what you can do instead?

There are two ways to avoid this kind of repetition (which I honestly see in a lot of writing). You can pick up a *thesaurus* and find different words for seat, or you can rearrange sentences to avoid the need for the word.

'Please sit down,' the teacher said.

I sat. The chair wasn't very comfortable. In fact, it was made of hard plastic and there was a bit of splintered wood on the back that was digging into me like the spine of a hedgehog.

'Whatever is the matter, Sophie?' The teacher asked as I wriggled, uncomfortable. 'Is there something wrong with your seat?'

Can you see how much better that second version of the writing is?

2. **Stick with your tenses.**

Another thing that I see a lot is tense hopping. I'm not talking about swapping from past to present narration, I'm talking about within a sentence.

He looked at the hole and, jumping over it, screamed,
landing on his sore ankle.

Can you see how the writer of this sentence (me) has started with an -ed suffix (looked), swapped to an -ing suffix (jumping), gone back to -ed (screamed) and then switched to -ing again at the end (landing).

Now read the same sentence, corrected.

He looked at the hole and jumped over it; he screamed as he
landed on his sore ankle.

The rule is, if you start a sentence with one suffix (tense) it is best to continue with that throughout the rest of the sentence.

Creating Atmosphere

Now you have your writing *technique* perfected, we can have some fun!

Atmosphere is a term used in literature to describe the *mood* of a piece of writing, which is usually created by how the author describes the setting and background but can also be created by sentence structure and word choice.

The creation of atmosphere will be important in your writing.

Imagine you are writing a light, happy story, you will want to give your reader that feeling of lightness and happiness throughout. You would not therefore, for example, set your story in a creepy graveyard, or use lots of words like rotting, stinking, mouldy etc.

You can show our reader what kind of story you are writing, through the use of different tools to create mood.

Different moods you might want to create (can you think of more?):

Alarming	Light
Brooding	Melancholy
Buoyant	Ominous
Comical	Oppressive
Confining	Relaxed
Cool	Romantic
Dark	Spooky
Fantastical	Suspenseful
Hopeful	Warm

Think of your favourite film. Filmmakers have lots of ways that they can create mood and build an atmosphere. They can move the camera around to show different perspectives, they can use music to create feelings of joy, excitement, suspense, fear. They can focus in on different sounds (insects scuttling, children laughing).

Watch this video of Frodo and his friends hiding from the Ringwraith in *Lord of the Rings* -

www.youtube.com/watch?v=2L0A2D7zV7A

In order to create tension, Peter Jackson shows you each tiny detail - we hear every sound the horse makes, the squelch of its hooves in the mud, the jangle of tack, the huff of its breath, we see the hooves, hard and sharp and black, in close up, from the perspective of the hobbits. We hear the breath of the Ringwraith and see the insects scuttling in response to its presence: snakes, centipedes and worms crawl on the hobbits. The soundtrack changes when Frodo thinks about putting on the ring, which, if he does, will make him invisible, but at the same time reveal his presence to the wraith.

Obviously, as writers we don't have a soundtrack, we can't use music, we can't pan the camera around, showing lots of different things happening. But there are tools we can use, to create an atmosphere which are just as effective.

To create atmosphere you, as a writer have a toolbox.

Tool one: Time of Day

Think about the time of day your story will take place. If you are writing a scary story, and it takes place at **night**, you can easily create a sense of menace, threat and uncertainty or, if it is a romance, you could create a sense of mystery, magic or intimacy.

A story set at **dawn** might have a feeling of possibility, of fresh starts, new beginnings.

Noon, could create a feeling of brightness and happiness, or of threat and climax (think of Westerns and 'high noon').

A story set at **dusk** (twilight) could have a sense of magic and strangeness or of melancholy or jaded cynicism (endings rather than beginnings).

In my novel *Savage Island,* when the teens start off on their adventure, they are full of optimism, confidence and possibility. The action therefore takes place during the daylight. They see moors, sparkling lochs, rabbits, seals, sheep, gulls, flowers, colour, babbling streams and so on.

When they discover the tooth in the box it is getting dark (twilight), the end of the day and that signifies the ending of all that positivity and optimism. They don't know what is going on, only that it seems bad.

As the story progresses, the teens are forced to move at night, for their own safety. At night on the island they encounter uneven ground, hidden rocks, bats, midges, hooting owls, there is no colour, it is cold and dark. This builds up a mood of fear, pessimism, distrust, doubt, uncertainty.

Tool two: The weather

Like the time of day, the weather is a useful tool for producing atmosphere.

It was a dark and stormy night ...

Look at these different forms of weather, what moods do you think they might evoke?

Weather	Mood
Sunny and warm	Warmth / joy
Grey skies	
Heavy fog	
Light rain / drizzle	
Heavy rain	
Light snow	
Blizzard	
Sleet	
Light breeze	
Strong wind / gale	
Hurricane	
Light cloud	
Light mist	
Tropical heat / humid	

You can use the weather to change the mood of the story and build up a mounting sense of tension. Again, the weather is important in the creation of atmosphere in Savage Island.

When things are going well, it is sunny and warm on the island, but as we get closer to the climax, it starts to rain, it gets cold, misty and wet and there are strong winds. The climactic battle takes place in fact, in rain and wind.

Tool three: Setting

Setting is an essential part of atmosphere. Setting is not the same as *world building* (which we discussed in an earlier chapter). I might plan to have my story take place in modern-day New York, but the *setting* might be an apartment building in the Upper East Side. Or I might have my story take place in a fantasy world, but the setting is a castle on a hill.

Your story's setting is the *time and place* where its events occur, and it should be thought through in a similar way to your characters in the sense that you should know your story's setting intimately, so that you can bring it to life for your readers. When writing your story, use every opportunity to really give us a sense of the sounds, sights, smells, touches and tastes of your character's environment.

Different settings create different atmospheres. And to emphasise how important setting is, I'd like you to consider this - what if the Harry Potter filmmakers had decided to set the films in a modern US high school, instead of in the Hogwarts you know and love?

Do you think that would have worked well?

Think about these different settings, what kind of story might take place in each?

Place	Mood	Story type
Abandoned warehouse	Eeriness, isolation, neglect.	Ghost story
Caribbean beach		
English beach in the rain		
Eiffel tower in Paris		
Speeding train		
Top of a mountain		
Castle		
Space station		
Expensive hotel		
Graveyard		
Fairground		

My own novel, *Windrunner's Daughter* was originally set in a future (dystopian) America long after a nuclear war has destroyed most of the country. When my character flew, we saw glimpses of familiar landmarks, and the climate she had to deal with was also familiar to the reader.

However, my editor suggested that the book would be better if it was set, not on earth at all, but on Mars.

I had to start again with my world building, setting the story on a Mars that has been partially terraformed, within a community that has been abandoned by earth (following the nuclear war that I envisioned for the original story) and has become patriarchal and religious (despite its scientific beginnings).

I had to do an awful lot of research into how exactly Mars could be terraformed, and how things like gravity (one third of Earth's), light levels and having two moons would affect the setting. I examined maps of Mars and read articles about what we know of the Martian landscape. I thought about what landmarks the characters would encounter and where they might live. I had to come up with ways that these people could make renewable oxygen masks and tanks, consider the materials they had to build, think about what they would grow and eat, how they would build their structures. Mars has these huge dust storms – how would these impact on the characters and story? I also considered what would happen if the partial terraforming had come up against native Martian life, perhaps rebirthing it.

You can imagine how much all of this changed the story. My main character (Wren) has a phobia of removing her mask, she has to contend with faulty breathing apparatus, biodomes, mega-storms, native organisms, terraforming equipment and lower gravity as well as the patriarchal attitudes of the society she lives in.

This new setting also changed the atmosphere, the sense of danger was enhanced due to the lower light levels, the cold and the oppressive nature of living inside a dome all the time.

Writing exercise	
Where would you set a ...	
Ghost story?	
Love story?	
Science fiction story?	
Crime story?	
Thriller?	
Fantasy story?	
Action adventure?	
Horror?	

Of course, different genres could share a setting. Imagine a hotel. You could set lots of different types of story in a hotel - Spy Thriller, Horror, Romance or Crime, for example.

But the hotel would be different in each story. There are famous hotels in film in different genres. The Overlook is the hotel in horror story *The Shining*, while Hotel Cipriani is the hotel in Spy thriller *Casino Royale*.

It is all going to be down to how you describe your hotel – which words you use to evoke atmosphere.

Can you picture these two, very different, hotels:

She hurried inside, her eyes soaking up the sumptuous sofas, gleaming floors and dazzling chandelier.

She gingerly stepped inside, her eyes widening at the sagging sofas, the filthy floor and dull, flickering light.

What sort of story is set in each hotel?

Hotel 1:

Hotel 2:

Who will your character meet?

Hotel 1:

Hotel 2:

The difference between the two hotels is in the different adjectives I relied upon to describe the setting. Hotel one – sumptuous, gleaming, dazzling. Hotel two – sagging, filthy, dull.

Word lists from which you can select adjectives can be useful reminders of the atmosphere you are aiming to create.

Here is the word list from which I selected the words to describe the first hotel -	
Sumptuous	Luxurious
Expensive	Lavish
Glittering	Plush
Shining	Grand
Gleaming	Spectacular
Dazzling	Abundant
Gorgeous	Sparkling
Opulent	Twinkling

Writing exercise
Write your own word lists for each of the following moods.

Spooky

Romantic

Alarming

Dark

Fantastical

Hopeful

Suspenseful

Relaxed / warm

When you are writing your story, think about the mood you want to create, then go to the word list you have created. You can select words from the list to help you describe the setting and make sure that the atmosphere is effective and consistent.

Remember to limit your adjective use to two or three per page if you can.

Tool four: Sensory description

You know about sensory description already, but did you know that it is a useful tool for creating atmosphere?

When you are writing your story, think about what your character might be focusing on, in their setting.

Look at the environment you are sitting in (perhaps it is your room, or a garden, or a classroom). Now think about a particular mood you would like to create in your story (perhaps a scary story). Picture your character sitting next to you, describing where you are. What sorts of things might catch their attention?

If you want to make the mood scary, your character might notice the shadows in the corners of your room, the cobwebs across the light bulb, the musty smell, the sound of dripping water, the feel of rough carpet on her knees, the sour taste in her mouth left over from lunch.

If you want to make the mood warm and comforting, your character might notice the brightly coloured duvet, the picture of flowers on the wall, the play of light on the curtains, the smell of perfume, the feel of warmth when they stretch their feet into a patch of sunlight, the taste of chocolate as she eats a piece.

So always think about the mood you want to create when you think about the sorts of things your character would notice when describing a place to the reader.

Tool five: Language

Using language in creative ways is the writer's way of replacing the music that a film director would add to a scene.

You will know some of the techniques that I am going to show you in this section, but some of them you will be learning for the first time. Honestly, there loads more techniques and rhetorical devices that I'm not going to go into here, as they would be a book all by themselves. I am just going to pick the ones I find the most useful to tell you about.

Alliteration

This is the one you were probably taught in school first. Alliteration is the occurrence of the same letter or sound at the beginning of adjacent, or closely-connected, words. In other words, it is starting words with the same letter.

Sickening silence.

Crying and coughing.

The sweet bird sang.

Bouncing ball.

Using alliteration in your work will immediately give it a certain poetry, a level of literariness, a professional feel that will impress your teachers, but did you know the letter or sound you choose can also impart a specific feel, or mood, to your piece of writing?

If you choose to repeat the letter S, this is called *SIBILANCE*. It can create a gentle or a sinister sound, depending on what the context is. Look at these two examples.

The soothing sound of the samurai's snores.

The snake slithered across the savannah.

Writing exercise
Can you write a sentence or paragraph with a sinister feeling (using lots of s-words)? And can you write a sentence with a soothing feeling (using lots of s-words)?

If you choose to repeat the sounds B, P, T or D these are called *PLOSIVES* (try saying just those letters – see how your lips create an *explosion* of breath). This creates the sensation of short sharp shock.

The balloon burst like a bomb in a beehive.

Writing exercise
Can you write a sentence or paragraph that imparts a feeling of shock (using lots of plosives)?

Assonance

Assonance is another one you might already know - this is when you repeat a vowel sound *inside* a word.

Take a look at this sentence from *Angel's Fury*. My main character is fleeing for her life and has hidden among some barley. It is a tense and frightening scene.

The barley rustles right beside me but I keep my eyes squeezed tight.

You might think that there isn't much 'poetry' in this line, but you would be wrong. In fact, I use alliteration (rustles right) and *two forms* of assonance, to make the line effective in creating a mood.

Read aloud the following words, taken from the sentence:

The bar<u>ley</u> <u>be</u>side <u>me</u> <u>keep</u> <u>squeezed</u>.

What vowel sound is repeated (think about the rhyme you can hear)?

And now look at these words:

<u>*Right* </u>*be*<u>*side*</u> *<u>I</u> <u>my</u> <u>eyes</u> <u>tight</u>*

What vowel sound is repeated (think about the rhyme you can hear)?

An ordinary reader would be unlikely to notice the assonance in the line, or how it affects them, they would just feel the increase in tension that I am aiming for, as their brain notices the poetry at a subconscious level.

Look again at the line. There is something odd about it. Would you normally say I keep my eyes squeezed <u>tight</u>, or I keep my eyes squeezed <u>shut</u>?

I deliberately chose the 'odd word', it does make sense, but it's not the phrase that the reader would normally use. This not only creates a feeling of 'oddness' and therefore discomfort in the reader, which I wanted, but in addition, the word 'tight' (in place of 'shut') continues the assonance that I have created in the earlier part of the line.

Consonance

This is when you repeat the consonant sound within words.

The <u>cl</u>i<u>ck</u>, <u>cl</u>ack of the train tra<u>ck</u>.

Dissonance

The opposite of assonance is dissonance. In music *dissonance* refers to discordant sounds or a lack of harmony in music, in writing it means deliberately *avoiding* repeated vowel sounds. You would be surprised how difficult it actually is to avoid all repeated vowel sounds.

Just look at the sentence above.

You would be surprised how difficult it actually is to avoid all repeated vowel sounds.

There are repeated vowel sounds in the word difficult, it and is. As well as the repeated -ow- sound in vowel and sounds. Not to mention the alliteration in actually and avoid!

To write a sentence that genuinely has no assonance (or alliteration) is not as simple as it sounds. When you are writing, your brain enjoys a certain lyricism, so you will often find yourself unconsciously choosing words and phrases that rhyme, or alliterate, because they 'sound better', especially if you are a big reader.

So why deliberately strip all poetry from a line? Again, it's down to that jarring effect that you might want to create for the reader.

If there are a lot of lines, or even paragraphs of lovely lyrical, poetic writing, to suddenly come across a line that cuts all of that off, will be a shock. You might want to use that shock in a piece of writing where the main character themselves is having a shock. That way the reader and character are equally surprised.

Onomatopoeia

The last language technique I am going to tell you, is again, one you likely already know – onomatopoeia. This is the formation of a word from a sound associated with what is named. In other words, this is a word that sounds like the thing it is describing.

Crash

Crack

Bang

Whistle

Cuckoo

Lullaby

Boom

Poof

Can you think of more?

These kinds of words are useful, again, in evoking a soundscape in the reader's mind. Using onomatopoeia means that your reader can literally hear what is happening on the page.

The crack of ice on the river.

Tool six: Sentence length

Varying the lengths of your sentence is important. It is a bit like pacing (we talked about the importance of highs and lows earlier) but at a sentence level. You need to give your reader breaks.

Writing nothing but long sentences can exhaust and bore your reader, writing nothing but short sentences can soon feel for the reader as if the writer is shouting at them full volume all the time.

Think about what is happening in your story before you choose how long your sentences will be. Long, leisurely sentences can give the reader a feeling of reflection or nostalgia. Shorter sentence can give the reader a feeling of urgency and danger.

When my characters are in danger, or are fleeing, I always shorten my sentences. In fact, the further they run, or the more afraid they are, the shorter the sentences get. Why?

Well, think about how you read aloud. Do you remember being told to take a long breath at a full-stop and a quick breath at a comma?

Now imagine that you have a piece of writing with lots of short sentences, you are taking long breaths more often. Imagine that your sentences are getting shorter and shorter, soon you are down to three words. Two words. One. What is your breathing doing?

Essentially you are panting. What do you do when you run fast, or are afraid? You pant.

By shortening the sentences, I am forcing the reader to pant along with the reader, to feel what they are feeling.

To illustrate the importance of varying your sentence length, there is nothing more effective than this piece of writing, Write Music, by Gary Provost, which can be found here:

https://laborenglishzone.blogspot.com/2016/04/write-music-by-gary-provost.html

Genre specific bits

By now you should have written something amazing so you might want to think about showing your story to others, perhaps even an agent or a publisher! In this section I am going to talk about what agents and publishers want.

Before you think about contacting an agent about your work, you need to know what you have actually written. Certain agents prefer to represent writers of certain genres or age-groups. You need to know where you fall, so you know who to contact (and who not to bother).

Here I am going to talk about the difference genres and age groups you can write for.

Some writers write with an audience in mind, others write their story first and then work out who they have written it for. This means I could have put this section here, or at the front of the book.

It is here. If you needed it earlier, I apologise.

I think that most people who are reading this book will be writing Mid-grade and above, so now I am going to start there.

Middle Grade (MG)

Middle-Grade novels are written for readers aged 9-12 years. Obviously, more advanced younger readers will be reading in this genre and honestly, some MG books are so fantastic, that a lot of adult readers will be reading them too. I loved *Harry Potter* (Rowling), *Mortal Engines* (Reeve), *Sabriel* (Nicholson), *Skullduggery Pleasant* (Landy), *Castle of Shadows* and *Artemis Fowl* (Colfer).

I loved many more, to be honest, but I can't list them all here, or the book will end up being another 100 pages long!

Within Mid-grade there is Lower Mid-grade (9-10 years) and Upper Mid-grade (11-12 years). Think the difference between *Charlie Turns into a Chicken* (Copeland) and *Percy Jackson* (Riordan).

In MG books the protagonist is usually in Primary School, or the first year or so of High School – think a maximum age of thirteen. This is because young readers tend to read aspirationally – they want to read about characters they would like to *be,* and young readers tend to look up to slightly older children.

However, if you make your protagonist too old, your readers won't be able to identify with them and, as you know, it is important for your reader to be able to identify with your character.

This means that 11/12 is the sweet spot for the protagonist's age in Lower MG and 12 /13 is the sweet spot for Upper MG.

Mid-grade books are most commonly narrated in third person, limited point of view.

He picked up the magic wand.

In terms of writing style, in MG books you will find a limited use of semi colons and colons, limited metaphor and simile (heavier focus on sensory description), simpler language, shorter paragraphs and chapters, more action, fast pace, no swearing, no sex / romance, no drugs, limited violence and minimal self-reflection.

The themes of MG literature tend to focus on the protagonist's friends, family, their immediate world and their relationship to it.

Young Adult (YA)

Young Adult (YA) novels are written for the age group 13 to 19 years. Again, more advanced younger readers and a lot of adult readers will also be reading this genre. I love so many YA books from *Dragonsong* (Macaffrey) to *The Wee Free Men* (Pratchett), *The Chaos Walking Trilogy* (Ness), *The Hunger Games* (Collins), *Graceling* (Cashore), *The Color Purple* (Walker) and *Throne of Glass* (Maas) – again, I could go on for *pages*.

Like MG, within YA there are two sub-categories, Teen and Upper YA. Teen is written for 13 to 15-year-olds, Upper YA for 16 to 19-year-olds.

Teen books tend to be 'cleaner' (less swearing, slightly less peril / less death and destruction – you wouldn't *usually* find teen horror nowadays – it would be classed as upper YA).

The age of the protagonist in YA literature tends to be around 16/17. There are a few reasons for this. First of all, this falls in the centre of the age range of its readers and means that it is most relatable, secondly this age falls between exams in the UK (after GCSEs before A-levels), so you don't have to worry about your character having to spend every spare minute revising (which would be a realistic portrayal of a 15/16 or 17/18-year-old), thirdly, this is often the age that young people are working out who they are and who they want to be and dealing with things like their own first loves and betrayals.

Something that distinguishes YA from Adult books is the voice of the protagonist. Young adult books have main characters whose voices are authentically young, with concerns, motivations and inner thoughts that are genuinely teenage. A teenager has different priorities, worries and thoughts than an adult (you wouldn't usually have a YA novel where the protagonist is worrying about paying the mortgage for example).

Young Adult books are most commonly narrated in third person limited, or first-person point of view.

I picked up the magic wand.

In terms of writing style, in YA books you will find heavier use of colons and semi colons, much use of metaphor and simile and more detailed description, more complex language, and longer paragraphs and chapters. You will usually also find some limited swearing, a romance / first love, drugs references are possible, there can be a lot of violence and the main character engages in self-reflection and analyses the meaning of events.

The themes of YA stories are usually centred on the protagonist discovering how he / she fits into the world beyond their friends and family. They are often issues-driven including such themes as first love and coming of age stories. YA is often typified by self-discovery, friendship, romance and identity.

New Adult

New Adult fiction bridges the gap between Young Adult and Adult genres. It typically features protagonists between the ages of 18 and 25.

The genre tends to focus on issues prevalent in the young adult genre as well as focusing on issues experienced by individuals between the area of childhood and adulthood, such as leaving home for university and getting a job.

This genre has not however, been particularly well received in the UK and it is not commonly found in bookshops.

Adult

I'm not going to say much about writing for adults here, as this book is aimed at young people. Needless to say; the main characters should be adults, with adult concerns, the voice should be that of an adult. You can be more 'literary' here, the pacing can (but does not have to be) slower and you can spend more time describing scenes.

Genres

Beyond age ranges, which, as we discussed earlier, will dictate your word count, you will have to know the genre your story falls into.

Why is it important to know your genre? The simple answer is that publishers sell to book shops and book shops (and libraries too) organise their shelves according to genre. Think of your local Waterstones. In there is a thriller section, a YA section, a sci-fi and fantasy section, a literary fiction section, a crime section, a horror section, a children's section, a non-fiction section and so on. If the publisher can't tell the book shop where they could shelve your book, the book shop is unlikely to buy it.

Publishers only want to buy books they can sell. They are businesses after all.

Why can't you write a Sci-fi-Western or a Romantic-Thriller, or a Fantasy-Crime? You can, of course you can (Joss Whedon's excellent *Firefly* is a Sci-fi Western but we know what happened to that), but it could limit how many publishers (and therefore agents) are willing to look at your work.

One of the reasons that it is nice to write MG or YA, is that these age-range categories are considered to be *genres* by shops, but within those you can write anything from romance to fantasy to horror to historical – it all gets shelved in the same place. So, if you want to write that crime story set in a Middle Earth, you can do it as a MG or YA novelist.

I myself have written YA paranormal romance, YA horror, YA dystopia, YA sci-fi and YA urban fantasy.

Genre list:

Genre	Features
Alternative history	Fiction set in a world where something fundamental has changed e.g. Hitler won the war or the library in Alexandria never burned down.
Biography	Narrative of a person's life.
Classic	Fiction that has become part of an accepted literary canon (widely taught in schools).
Crime	Story is driven by the need to find out who committed a crime.
Dystopia	Warnings about a near future gone wrong, features an oppressive regime. Used to draw attention to real-world issues regarding society, environment, politics, economics, religion, psychology, ethics, science, and/or technology.
Fantasy	Based on magic rather than science, often in a world other than our own.
Gothic	Fiction mixing themes of horror, romance, and death.
Historical	Fiction set in our past.
Horror	The story is driven by fear (every decision driven by fear).
Magical realism	A story in which magical elements blend with the real world. The magical elements draw on fable, folktale and myth. For example, a character may discover a genie in a bottle.
Memoir	Factual story that focuses on a significant relationship between the writer and a person, place, or object; reads like a short novel.
Mystery	Fiction dealing with the revealing of secrets.
Realistic / Contemporary realism	True to life.
Romance	The story is driven by love (every decision driven by love).
Satire	Vices, follies, abuses and shortcomings are held up to ridicule.

Genre	Features
Science fiction (sci-fi)	Speculative fiction, 'the literature of change', will often include outer space, alien worlds, scientific advances or science that hasn't been invented yet. There are clear rules about how things work (physics, chemistry, biology).
Spy	Fiction involving espionage.
Superhero	Fiction involving crime fighters with supernatural powers.
Suspense	Fiction involving harm about to befall a person or group and the attempts made to evade the harm.
Swashbuckler	Story based on a time of swordsmen, pirates and ships, and other related ideas, usually full of action
Thriller	A story that holds reader interest by employing a high degree of intrigue, adventure, or suspense.
Urban fantasy	Set in a modern city, but fantasy creatures live in the city and interact with the population.
Western	Fiction set in the American Old West frontier.

These are what I would call the main genres.

Within these are dozens of sub-genres. Look at *Fantasy* for example, under that umbrella there is Epic / high fantasy, Hard fantasy, Historical fantasy, Prehistoric fantasy, Medieval fantasy, Wuxia, Low fantasy, Urban fantasy, Paranormal romance, Comic fantasy, Contemporary fantasy, Dark fantasy, Fantasy of manners, Heroic fantasy, Magic realism, Mythic, Paranormal fantasy, Shenmo fantasy, Superhero fantasy and Sword and sorcery.

Under *science-fiction* there is Alien invasion, Post-apocalyptic, Cyberpunk, Biopunk, Nanopunk, Postcyberpunk, Steampunk, Atompunk, Clockpunk, Dieselpunk, Solarpunk, aka Hopepunk, my own Junk punk (*Phoenix Rising*), Dystopian, Hard science fiction, Military science fiction, Parallel universe, aka alternative universe, Alternative history, LitRPG, Scientific romance,

Social science fiction, Soft science fiction, Space opera, Portal fantasy aka Isekai and Accidental travel.

Under *Crime* there is Hard-boiled, Police procedural, Cosy, Whodunnit, Caper, Legal, Detective, Locked room and Howcatchem.

Don't worry, for now, about all the sub genres, just focus on the main genre and target audience when approaching agents.

Finally, I am going to give you a few genre-specific top tips.

My top tips for writing Horror

1. The setting should be a place with its own rules, often isolated, like an island (*Savage Island*), a castle (*Dracula, Cruel Castle*), or a place otherwise cut off from the world (*Whiteout, The Dome, The Fog*).

2. You must make your reader care about your characters.

3. Your characters must have something to lose (otherwise a heroic sacrifice means nothing).

4. Use real fears to make the fear of your monsters relatable: spiders, doctors / surgeons / dentists, darkness, clowns.

5. Or you could subvert expectations and take something that wouldn't normally be scary and turn it on your reader: children (*Children of the damned*), toys (*Frozen Charlotte, Chucky*), games (*Say her name*), pets (*Pet Cemetery*), cars (*Christine*), books (*Evil Dead*), social media (*unfriended*), phones (*Cell*), technology (*Terminator*).

6. Add as much suspense as possible.

7. Add twists and turns - The monster might not be what we are expecting, the main character might not be who we thought they were, an attack could be from an unexpected direction.

8. A real horror story will contain gore, but do lead up to this, I don't recommend writing a non-stop schlock-fest.

9. Consider using your story to include a message, fear has a lasting impact, so your message will likely remain with your reader. Think about what you want to say: respect the environment, don't rock the boat, be responsible with technology, pay attention to your children, just because you can doesn't mean you should etc.

My top tips for writing Dystopia

1. Dystopia is very often issue driven. Decide on your issue / message first and base your world-building around what the world would be like if that issue was never solved, and things went too far.

> For example, if your issue is racism, you could imagine a world where the whole structure of society depended on the paleness of your skin, if your issue is school shootings, you could imagine a world where all children are taken from their parents at five and put into maximum security compounds to learn, if your issue is plastic surgery / body modification you could imagine a world in which everyone has to have plastic surgery in order to fit in with a government established ideal of beauty and so on.

2. Make the community / society frightening by including the following -
   a. Dehumanisation
   b. Totalitarian government
   c. Environmental disaster
   d. A cataclysmic decline in society

3. Draw contrasts between the privileges of the ruling class and the existence of the working class.

4. Your characters could be battling to overthrow or escape the totalitarian regime that controls their lives. Penalties for transgressions should be severe.

My top tips for writing Crime

While in Dystopia world-building comes first, in Crime, the plot comes first. The story should fit the crime.

1. Decide on the crime you want to happen and fit your story around that. Your crime must be believable and solvable with rational scientific methods.

2. Before you start writing, decide - What was the crime? Who is the victim? Who is the criminal? Who are the suspects? How was it done? Where was it done? Why was it done? What clues will you leave? What red herrings will you leave? How is it discovered?

3. Don't get bogged down in back story or go off on tangents.

4. Don't try to fool the reader - clues should be revealed as the detective finds them.

5. Don't use improbable disguises, twins, accidental solutions, or supernatural solutions.

6. Do know what the reader is expecting and turn it into something they don't – that is the basic purpose of crime fiction.

7. Introduce detective and culprit early on and remember that the best villains in mysteries are often those closest to the detective.

8. The detective should be admirable (clever, determined), relatable (with fears and foibles) and their fears (e.g. heights, snakes) should be an obstacle to unmasking the villain.

9. The villain must be capable of committing the crime (physically and emotionally), be as easily dismissible as possible and have a believable motive.

My top tips for writing Science fiction

Science fiction stories are often driven by the need for change in the world. They can be metaphors for the things going on in our own world, and a long time ago were a vehicle for demanding change that could escape censorship (I'm only writing about aliens, sir).

1. Remember that science fiction is the literature of change so, make sure you finish with a changed world.
2. Do include science and technology but …
3. *Do your research.* You don't want to base your idea on debunked ideas, old science, or incorrect assumptions. This is particularly true if you are writing hard sci-fi.
4. Stick to the rules of physics.
5. Consider the human connection to / reaction to technology, alien races etc.
6. Don't include magic (this is fantasy, and the two genres don't mix well).
7. Don't let too much science get in the way of a good story.

My top tips for writing Fantasy

While Science-Fiction is usually *revolutionary* (it demands change) Fantasy is commonly *reactionary*, either looking back to a golden age that the protagonist wishes to re-establish (for example restoring the good royal family as in *Throne of Glass*), or protecting the existing golden age from an external threat (e.g. the Dark One in *The Wheel of Time*). This is one reason that the two genres do not mesh well.

Another reason is that fantasy is about magic, while science fiction centres on physics.

1. Do include magic but ...
2. Give your magic rules and restrictions.
3. Highlight the golden age to which your characters want to return, or the awesomeness of the world that they are protecting.
4. Allow yourself to put twists on familiar fantasy figures (wizards, elves, dwarves, orcs, magical creatures etc)
5. Don't include anachronistic modern technology.
6. Don't let your world building overtake your story.

My top tips for writing Romance

Romance stories are driven by a character's need for a relationship. The character wants love, and the story will be about the obstacles they face on the way to securing the loving relationship they need.

1. Don't write a MG romance.

2. You can include sex in a YA romance story but be careful!

3. Put obstacles in the way of the romance – make your characters have to fight for it.

4. Make your characters likable and ordinary (some of my recent favourite romances include very ordinary looking women – Jenny Crusie's *Bet Me* – or women over the age of forty). It is how they face their challenges will make them special.

5. Don't rely on stereotypes.

6. Don't make it all about 'the boy' - remember the Bechdel test

   (The Bechdel test, is a measure of the representation of women in fiction. It asks whether a work features at least two women who talk to each other about something other than a man).

7. Don't forget the action.

My top tips for writing Comedy

Comedy books are funny and often involve a knotty problem that the character must undo.

There are a lot of funny MG books, but far fewer funny YA novels. Personally, I think there is a huge gap in the market for YA comedies aimed at teenage boys. Right now, I can only think of one: *The Gifted, the Talented and Me* by Will Sutcliffe.

If you can write good comedy (for boys), then publishers will snap you up. But how do you write funny …

1. Do know your audience and subvert their expectations – be unexpected
2. Use extremes
3. Include dark humour or satire
4. Play with slapstick (who doesn't enjoy a good injury?)
5. Use delays and understatements
6. Include jokes about bodily functions – kids love those!
7. Think about how situations might be made funny.
8. Let your characters make mistakes, do absurd things and use funny gestures or phrases.

After you've written your story

Editing

Once you have written your story or novel you will need to polish it. Editing is essential. I know, you probably hate editing, many people do, but not me, I love to see something I have written getting better and better.

What is editing?

Editing is rewriting, polishing, making sure that your story, or book, is as good as it can possibly be.

Before you edit, you need to take a break from your work. I know, you don't want to. Not only are you desperate to get this part over with, but time away from your writing feels like time wasted. *Honestly* it isn't!

This is one of the most useful things you can do for your own writing. If you start editing the second you've written '*The End*', then you will be too close to your work. You won't see the places it doesn't work, or where the pace lags and every word will feel too valuable to cut.

Time and distance mean that you feel less attached to the work. The longer you spend away from it, the more it will feel almost as if it was written by someone else when you go back to it and the easier you will find to critique it. You will find yourself thinking, 'did I really write that?', and 'gosh that's terrible' or 'I can't believe I didn't notice that before.'

So, take as much time away as you can. You might have a deadline and can't take that time away, but if there is no deadline, then give yourself as much time off as you can bear. Go and write something else perhaps, keep honing your craft. *Then* go back and edit your writing.

When editing, the first thing you need to do is read the whole story. Anywhere that you think 'wow, that's really good, well done me, I can't believe I wrote such a great scene!' should be highlighted with blinking gold stars where possible. Remind yourself that you can do this. You have your moments of awesomeness. Writing is your *thing*.

Anywhere however, where you are bored, or you find yourself skipping, that needs to be highlighted in red because you are either going to cut it altogether, or rewrite.

Check that you still love the characters, or does anyone annoy you? Do any of the characters feel redundant, can they perhaps be merged? Does the hero need three friends, or would it be better with just two?

Check that the setting makes sense and that you haven't broken any rules in your world-building.

Once you've done the first overall read, read it again, looking for detail problems – have you slipped into passive voice, or telling anywhere? Is there repetition? Is there a word that you didn't realise you relied on too much?

Make notes on your document and in a notebook beside you.

I use *Microsoft Word* for both writing and editing. The lovely thing about writing on the computer is that you can save different versions of your document. You can make cuts, put the writing that you have cut in a separate document titled 'cut stuff', read your story with and without the cut and decide which version is better. Or you can use your 'cut stuff' in scenes (or even another novel) later on. It doesn't feel as if you are throwing things away if you have your 'cut stuff' file.

Of course, I find that 90% of my 'cut stuff' file does end up being deleted, but it's a nice buffer to have it there, still accessible.

It is also worth remembering that you don't have to edit alone. You can give your work to other people to critique.

Ideally you want someone with an impartial, critical eye.

Obviously, your parents would be a good first port of call but do remember that they love you and, if your work is terrible, will be unlikely to tell you so. The same goes for your best friend, or children (either your own of those in a local school), who rarely give honest feedback, as they so love to please visiting authors (this is why many agents shudder when they receive a covering letter that says – I gave my story to the local primary school and all the children loved it, so I know it must be good).

A critique partner or writing group can be really helpful in improving your writing, by giving you a valuable outside perspective and perhaps offering suggestions and reassurance.

Your teacher (if you are still in school) might be willing to help you edit your work or put you in touch with another enthusiastic creative writer so you can partner up. Or you could ask at your local library if they have a writing group you could join (many do – and they're free).

Alternatively, you could go online and publish somewhere like Wattpad. This social platform lets authors share stories with millions of readers for free. Many authors publish to get feedback or gauge traction for titles or offer the first few chapters of a longer work as a teaser.

There is a website here with a comprehensive list of places you could find an online critique partner. If you are not eighteen, *please* do not contact any of these without parental guidance.

thewritelife.com/find-a-critique-partner/

If you don't want to work with a critique partner or you want more professional feedback, there are also professional organisations that will read your work (for a fee) and provide you with a report, or annotations on your manuscript which tell you what you are doing right, where you are going wrong and how you can fix it.

The two that I would recommend are *Cornerstones Literary Consultancy* and *The Writing Coach*.

https://cornerstones.co.uk

https://thewritingcoach.co.uk

However, there are many more, and some writers do this privately. Again, if you are under 18, do get a parent to help you search for the right partner.

If you want to take this writing business seriously, you could also join organisations. The SCBWI, for example (the Society of Children's Book Writers and Illustrators) is a fantastic group for people who want to write for young people. They have critique groups, online groups, bulletins, books, podcasts, workshops, events, advice, competitions, awards and grants … they're great. And cost about £70 for a year's membership.

How to find an agent

Once your story or novel is polished to perfection you might decide that you want to get it published. Seeing your book on the shelves of a bookshop between Patrick Ness and Terry Pratchett (I'm 'Pearce') is one of the best things in the world, and there are lots of publishing houses that you can approach to make this dream come true. Big names like *Penguin Random House*, *Harper Collins*, or *Macmillan*, mid-range ones like *Stripes*, or *Egmont* and smaller, independent presses like *Telos* or UCLAN.

The first step in being published however, is often to find yourself an agent who will work on your behalf to sell your book.

What is an agent?

An agent is the person who will sell your book to a publisher, help you get a good deal, help you with edits and be your cheerleader. Film stars have agents and so do writers. We're cool that way!

Wait, do I really need an agent, can't I just go it alone?

Sure, you can go it alone. You can even approach publishers with your work directly. Most publishers (like *Penguin Random House*) don't accept unsolicited submissions. This means that they only take manuscripts from agents. So, if you decide to try and get published without an agent, the first thing you're doing is limiting the number of publishers who will be looking at your work.

Here is a list of publishers who at the time of writing (Summer 2021) would look at unsolicited manuscripts. Check their websites for submission guidelines.

- Andersen Press
- Ransom Publishing
- Buster Books
- Candy Jar Books
- Walker Books
- Dinosaur Books
- Fledgling Press
- Floris Books
- Flying Eye Books
- The Quarto Group
- Sweet Cherry Publishing
- Maverick Books
- Mogzilla
- Imagine That Publishing
- Wacky Bee Books
- Birlinn Limited
- Picadilly Press
- Booklife
- Everything with Words
- Strident Publishing
- Matthew James Publishing

An agent can not only get your work in front of the right publisher, but will also help you with edits, listen to ideas, keep you on track and make sure you get a good deal and that your contract is fair and right for you.

I have 'gone it alone' and sold a couple of books, but when I signed with my current agent, she immediately negotiated me a better deal for me. Agents take 15% of earnings, but if they get more money for you, they pay for themselves.

I want an agent, but there are so many, which do I choose?

There are a lot of agents, but they don't all represent the same kind of writer. I'd recommend getting the *Writer's and Artist's Yearbook* (for the current year). Go through and narrow down the agents that are looking for what you are writing (there's no point submitting to an agent who only represents Adult Crime novels if you're writing Middle-Grade Fantasy).

Another way you could find the right agent is to look at writers who have published similar things – who represents them? Once you've got yourself a list, then you can start stalking! Look at the agency website, look for blogs or articles by the agents you like, follow them on Twitter and Instagram – see what they love, what they loathe, if you click with their voice and style. Perhaps even tweet them a relevant question, or lightly and politely engage, so that when your manuscript lands on their desk they may remember your name.

Is it easy to get an agent?

Honestly, no. It's very difficult. Agents have thousands of writers asking them to take them on. They pick very few of these and only the writers who send them something they really love and know they can sell. On the plus side, if you are picked from the slush-pile by an agent then you know you're a great writer, and on your way to being published.

I've narrowed it down to twenty I like, do I submit to all these?

What I would recommend is that you should break them up into groups of five. Submit to your first five. Hopefully, you'll get one asking for your full manuscript but, if not, you might still be lucky and get some feedback. If you do, you can act on it before sending to your next five and then your next five and so on. Save your favourite five till last, because by then your work will be even more polished. One an agent has said no, they are unlikely to want to see the same novel from you again, even if you've rewritten it.

How do I approach them, what do I send?

Always look at the agency website (or call if they haven't got a website). Most agents like a covering letter, synopsis and the first three chapters, and you can usually email your submission in. Some have different requirements, however, so check first. And make sure you send to your carefully selected, named agent!

Always check that you haven't accidentally mis-named the agent, especially if you're copying and pasting from one email to another. You'd be amazed, but my agent really does get emails asking her for representation, addressed to rivals!

Synopsis

A synopsis is basically a one-page book summary (you essentially wrote the synopsis on page 135).

A synopsis is not a blurb, it isn't there to tease your agent and make them want to read on to find out what happens next - it should contain all the high points of your novel, clearly showing the narrative arc and emotional journey of your main character.

Why do agents need a synopsis?

They use it to check that the story is working structurally and that everything makes sense. If a synopsis is confusing, it may well be that the story will come across that way too. Aim to be short, sweet and to the point.

How should I present my synopsis?

Standard UK industry requirement is one A4 page, with plenty of white space around paragraphs. Usually, a synopsis is Times New Roman, 12 point, but single-line spacing. Names should be capitalised the first time they are used.

What should I include?

Paragraph one: Briefly set the scene and introduce your protagonist.

Paragraph two: Describe the inciting event – what propels the character into the problem.

Paragraph three: How does the protagonist explore the situation / attempt to overcome their problem?

Paragraph four: What unexpected (but not totally out of the blue) thing occurs to tip the character into peril and/or despair?

Paragraph five: In what way does the protagonist dig themselves out of danger and emerge triumphant (or not).

Final paragraph: Summarise the story in terms of its themes and central messages.

I can't make it any shorter, do you have any other tips?

I sometimes pretend that I'm telling my story to a friend in the pub (short attention span, not actually very interested). What are the high points I tell them?

The difference between a synopsis and a blurb?

The blurb is what you get on the back of the book – the couple of paragraphs that sells the book to prospective readers. This is also what can go in the covering letter (if it's short enough). It should be a *teaser*.

Savage Island <u>blurb</u>

When reclusive millionaire Marcus Gold announces that he's going to be staging an "Iron Teen" competition on his private island in the Outer Hebrides, teenagers Ben, Lizzie, Will, Grady and Carmen sign up – the prize is one million pounds ... each.

But when the competition begins, the group begin to regret their decision. Other teams are hunting their competitors. Can the friends stick together under such extreme pressure to survive?

When lives are at stake, you find out who you can really trust ...

A Red Eye horror novel for teens, this gripping YA thriller story is full of fast-paced action.

WINNER OF THE WIRRAL BOOK AWARD 2019

Savage Island <u>synopsis</u>

BEN is used to following LIZZIE, he's been doing it all his life, so when Lizzie suggests that they enter the Iron-Teen endurance competition announced by billionaire MARCUS GOLD he can't say no. And why would he? Especially with a prize of £1m.

When their team is allocated a place, Ben, his younger brother WILL, Lizzie and their friends GRADY, and CARMEN set off to Gold's private island. While they are crossing the causeway to reach the starting point, their packs are soaked, and their phones destroyed.

When they arrive, the team is disappointed to find that the competition (which consists of orienteering, puzzle solving and endurance) has already begun. At each checkpoint, the teams must remove the 'treasure' from inside a box and replace it with something of equal value. At the first checkpoint there is a locked box containing a human tooth. Later Carmen is attacked, and her hand cut off. Horrified, the team realise that the boxes must all contain body parts. Unable to leave the island, the group race towards the end of the course, hunted all the way, in the hope that there will be help at the finish line.

At the final checkpoint, there is a battle in which Carmen manages to stab the boy who cut off her hand. Finally, the team discovers a secret staircase leading to a room with a bank of monitors. There they are informed that a huge sum of money is available to just one of them – on condition they kill someone on their team. Gold believes that psychopaths make the best business leaders; he wants psychopaths that he can control. Ben confesses that the psychopath Gold is interested in must be his brother. While they are trying to work out what to do, Grady murders the injured Carmen to win the prize for himself. Will turns on Grady, but, to Ben's surprise, does not kill him. Eventually they work out how to escape and flee into a warren of tunnels.

Ben, Lizzie and Will manage to find their way to the causeway. However, tragedy strikes when Will gets stuck in quicksand, and they are unable to pull him free. Lizzie sets off swimming and Ben follows her. Unfortunately, the currents are too strong, and they are swept apart. Ben wakes on a familiar beach surrounded by bodies. Finally, Grady appears, and tells Ben that Gates has given him his first job.

This is a horror story about love and friendship, which asks the fascinating question, what would you do for £1 million?

How to write your own blurb

If you've read all of this book, you'll know that your main character will have a central problem to solve - a goal, with high stakes for failure. Now you know this, you should be able to write down a central, one-line problem for your story.

For example, for some of my novels:

Windrunner's Daughter – how will Wren save her mother's life, while obeying the rules of the cruel patriarchy?

Wavefunction – how will Kane find his way home when he ends up in an alternative universe?

Savage Island – how will the teenaged heroes survive when they find themselves on an island of psychopaths?

Phoenix Rising – how will Toby save his pirate father when he is captured by the authorities?

Weight of Souls – how can Taylor solve the murder of a boy she hates, when it looks like an accident?

The Girl on the Platform – how can Bridget find a kidnapped girl, when no-one believes that she saw anything?

Raising Hell – how can Ivy stop a mysterious cabal from taking over the country by raising zombies?

Cruel Castle – how can Grady escape a castle filled with lethal traps, and bring down the evil Marcus Gold?

Once you have done that think, what is the core *message* you wanted to convey:

> *Windrunner's Daughter* – Girls are just as good as boys.

> *Wavefunction* – Free will makes us human.

> *Savage Island* – What is the nature of trust?

> *Phoenix Rising* – Growing up is hard, but essential.

> *Weight of Souls* – Bullying is wrong.

> *The Girl on the Platform* – Trust yourself.

> *Raising Hell* – Blame achieves nothing.

> *Cruel Castle* – Continues trust theme of Savage Island.

In order to write a simple blurb, take your one core problem, give enough information to flesh out the detail, so a reader knows what is going to happen. Finish with a pithy quote that picks up your central message / theme. For example, Phoenix Rising could be something like:

In a future world destroyed by a volcano and buried in trash, Toby lives with his father on a pirate ship. Never allowed to set foot on dry land, for his own safety, he is treated like a younger brother by all the other pirates. But when his father is captured by the authorities, Toby will have to team up with his worst enemy and go on land to save him.

Growing up is hard, it's even harder when no-one thinks you should.

Covering Letter

Once you have a synopsis and a blurb, you can write the letter to the specific agent you've decided to approach.

Presentation of the letter should be similar to that of the synopsis: Times New Roman, 12-point spacing, single line layout. Make sure that you include all of your contact details at the top of the letter, allowing the agent to easily get in touch with you.

It's good to offer all the crucial information about your submission at the top of the letter, mention what you are including, reveal your title, genre and age range. You should also include the word count.

Something like this:

Dear Catherine,

I am seeking representation for my young adult horror novel, Savage Island, which is 65,000 words long and aimed at older teenagers. I include my synopsis and first three chapters for your interest.

Do personalise the letter and give an indication of why you're targeting this particular agent or publishing house. You might explain that you read an article about them or attended a talk they gave, that you have looked at their website and know they specialise in books for your target age range, or even that you have read a book by a writer they represent. Ideally, you want something to show you've done your research rather than picked them at random. The more particular your reason the better.

For example:

I attended a talk you gave last year about the importance of writing fantastic characters and found it incredibly inspiring. I put your ideas into my own protagonist, a boy who is trying to survive against all odds.

A single paragraph outlining the plot should follow. The idea is to provide a tantalising taster, but you don't need to go into detail. This is where your blurb comes in.

I describe my novel as a cross between Lord of the Flies and The Apprentice. It's about teenagers who are trying to win a million pounds by completing a geocaching competition on a remote island. However, not all is what it seems. I ask the question what would you do to protect your family and what would you do for £1 million?

Talk about why you wrote the book, what drew you to the subject, genre or audience.

My novel deals with the monsters in the human psyche, which is a subject that has always interested me. I chose to write this into a geocaching competition as it is a sport enjoyed by all ages and walks of life.

Do think if there is anything particularly interesting about your own personal story – agents and publishers are always seeking a hook with which they can sell a writer (for example JK Rowling wrote Harry Potter in a coffee shop while she was a single mum).

This story of survival is particularly important to me as I personally survived a shark attack two years ago.

This bit isn't true by the way, don't worry about me, but if you can, think of a true story that is just as good!

Again, if you can, demonstrate that this is not your only project.

While this is a stand-alone story, I have already started writing a new novel, an urban fantasy titled Raising Hell, which is equally dark and thrilling.

Do talk about your work and hobbies, the agent wants to get a sense of you as a person and do mention any particular writing qualifications you might have, for example competition wins or previous publication history.

I have had seven novels published and am a winner of Undiscovered Voices, the Leeds Book Award, the Wirral Book Award and the Cheshire Schools Book Award. In my free time, I enjoy films, theatre, reading, and walking in the Forest near my home. However, I have two children, so my free time is strictly limited!

Let the agent or publisher know if you are sending your work out to more than one institution, it is only polite.

For your information, I am submitting at this time to a total of five agents, a carefully selected group who I am excited to send my work to.

Finally, proofread! Grammar and punctuation mistakes may put agents off your work. And good luck!

The last thing to say is, don't be disheartened if (when) you get rejected. Something that all authors must develop is a thick skin. From Charles Dickens to JK Rowling, to Stephen King, we have all been rejected dozens and dozens of times, but it only takes one yes, one person to love your work and you're away.

And remember that not all rejections are about the quality of your work. The agent you're applying to might have a full roster, and just can't take anyone else on right now, or they might already have five vampire / werewolf romances that they're trying to sell and can't take on another one. Or they might love your work, but know they can't sell it, as your story idea is out of fashion, or a big name has just sold a similar storyline.

I once met a woman who had written a novel and who gave up after a single rejection, never to try again. I could scarcely believe it. It was an amazing rejection too – the agent had sent her pages of editorial notes. She didn't know that this was practically unheard of and meant that she was very clearly almost there until I told her so!

Authors must be thick skinned, stubborn, persistent and filled with self-belief. Yet most of us are riddled with self-doubt due to all the rejections, criticisms and bad reviews. We're an odd sort of breed.

Self-publishing

Getting an agent and a book deal with a traditional publisher is the holy grail for most writers, it means you've got past the quality control gatekeepers and there's a good chance you'll see your name on the shelf of Waterstones or WHSmith. But it isn't the be-all and end-all.

Many authors now are going down the self-publishing route. If you do decide to self-publish you do give up the kudos of being traditionally published and the weight of the publishing company Sales and Marketing department, which means you have to do all your own marketing and the hard work of getting the book into shops, or otherwise into reader's hands.

However, self-publishing no longer has the stigma that it once had. The advantages are that you can keep creative control of your work (choosing your own title, own cover design, own blurb and edits) and, more importantly for many writers, most of the money you get from selling it, which is an attractive proposition. With a traditional book deal you usually get around 10% of a book sale, whereas KDP Select (self-publishing with Amazon), offers you 60%.

It also means you can publish on your own timeline. With a traditional publisher it can take up to *two years* from signing your contract to seeing your book published (by which point your family is beginning to wonder if you're delusional). If you self-publish somewhere like Amazon, you can be making money soon after finished editing.

If you do self-publish however, do be prepared to spend some money to make your work as professional as possible. If your work is riddled with grammatical errors and spelling mistakes for example, you won't get anyone to pick up your second book.

So do consider hiring a professional editing service. Do also budget for someone to do you a nice cover design and perhaps some advertising.

With self-publishing you could do ebook only or print on demand.

If you want to know more about self-publishing you could look at

https://selfpublishing.com/self-publishing/

Vanity publishing

Vanity publishing is where you pay a publishing company to publish your book for you. These publishing houses often pretend to be reputable, traditional publishers, and will offer you a contract, hidden in which are a lot of costs to you, the author.

Vanity press publishing, also called subsidy publishing, differs from self-publishing in that the author assumes all the risk and pays the publisher for everything. The editing, formatting, cover design, and even marketing the book are paid for by the author through the various packages offered when an author signs up.

Some of these companies never intend to get your book in front of readers, their aim is to extract as much money as possible from you. They are scammers.

I know someone who spent several thousand on vanity publishing and hasn't seen a penny in return. It is to be avoided.

If a publishing company offers you a book deal and then asks you for money, they are a vanity publisher, and you should run away as fast as you can.

Writing prompts

I am going to end this book with some fun creative writing prompts. I could go on forever, talking about contracts and marketing and all that stuff that comes after you've got your agent and publisher (or have self-published) but that isn't what this book is about. This book is about writing your story like a professional.

Now you know pretty much everything that I do, I can't wait to see your name on a book-shelf next to mine!

'What have you done?' the headmaster bellowed, all eyes now turned to me as I stood over the …

It was the first time I saw a …

I have something to tell you, the man said, and you're not going to like it ….

The box sat on my doorstep, quietly ticking …

It was mid-day but the sky was black …

This is the saddest story I have ever heard …

It was an ordinary Thursday when the professor said …

The egg started to crack …

'I can't believe it,' Aunt Mandy said, holding up the letter …

I thought the attic was empty, but it wasn't …

The footsteps stopped outside my door …

The door, which had always been locked, now stood open …

As I stared at my reflection, it moved all by itself and said …

Congratulations, the letter said, you have won …

Most of all, remember to have fun writing.

Index

Printed in Great Britain
by Amazon

57409243R00165